MUDRAS
and
CRYSTALS

THE ALCHEMY
OF ENERGY PROTECTION

SABRINA MESKO

AUTHOR OF INTERNATIONAL BESTSELLER
HEALING MUDRAS

BY SABRINA MESKO

HEALING MUDRAS
Yoga for Your Hands
Random House - Original edition

POWER MUDRAS
Yoga Hand Postures for Women
Random House - Original edition

MUDRA - GESTURES OF POWER
DVD - Sounds True

CHAKRA MUDRAS DVD set
HAND YOGA for Vitality, Creativity and Success
HAND YOGA for Concentration, Love and Longevity

HEALING MUDRAS
Yoga for Your Hands - New Edition

HEALING MUDRAS - New Edition in full color:
Healing Mudras I. ~ For Your Body
Healing Mudras II. ~ For Your Mind
Healing Mudras III. ~ For Your Soul

POWER MUDRAS
Yoga Hand Postures for Women - New Edition

MUDRA THERAPY
Hand Yoga for Pain Management and Conquering Illness

YOGA MIND
45 Meditations for Inner Peace, Prosperity and Protection

MUDRAS FOR ASTROLOGICAL SIGNS
Volumes I. ~ XII.

MUDRAS FOR ARIES, TAURUS, GEMINI, CANCER, LEO, VIRGO, LIBRA, SCORPIO, SAGITTARIUS, CAPRICORN, AQUARIUS, PISCES
12 Book Series

LOVE MUDRAS
Hand Yoga for Two

The Holistic Mudra Series

MUDRAS *and* CRYSTALS

SABRINA MESKO

Book One

The material contained in this book has been written for informational
purposes and is not intended as a substitute for medical advice,
nor is it intended to diagnose, treat, cure, or prevent disease.
If you have a medical issue or illness, consult a qualified physician.

A MUDRA Hands™ Book
Published by Mudra Hands Publishing
an Imprint of

ARNICA PRESS
www.ArnicaPress.com

Copyright © 2021 Sabrina Mesko

Photos by Mara
Crystal Photos by Sabrina
Symbols and Illustrations Kiar Mesko

ON THE COVER:
Mudra for Mastering Freedom

Printed in the United States of America

First MUDRA Hands Publishing Edition
February 2021

Manufactured in the United States of America

ISBN: 978-1-7352446-4-8

*For all who Recognize and Love
the Sacred Spirits of the Magnificent Crystals…*

Vera Cruz Amethyst resting on a Golden Healer Quartz Barnacle

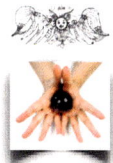

CONTENTS

X. ASTRAL PROTECTION SHIELD 163

Mudra for:

MUDRA INDEX

FOREWORD

It has been precisely twenty-one years since my very first book, titled *Healing Mudras* entered this world. At that time, my book was the first in depicting the ancient and wondrous Mudra technique. Since then, I have written many more books on this fascinating subject and embarked on an incredible journey of sharing this knowledge with all who felt a deep curiosity and passion for the ancient hand gestures.

The fact that such a mighty self-healing tool is freely available in your hands is clear evidence that we hold all the answers and solutions to our challenges within our very own being. The greatest marvel and puzzle to uncover and unveil is You. To properly practice the Mudra Technique it is essential to hold the positions with utmost precision and have a clear intention for a specific purpose. It is only when mastering these aspects that you can overcome a challenge on command, at the decisive moment when you need assistance, empowerment and answers to your deep, soul searching questions.

In the past few decades, I have dedicated many years to refining the teaching techniques for the proper Mudra practice and developed specific applications of Mudra Therapy technique to help with various persistent challenges one may face. I have paired Mudras with a variety of other complimentary healing modalities and have created numerous private mentorship courses for all Mudra seekers who longed to experience a deeper practice and enjoy far reaching benefits. Nowadays, my certified Mudra Teachers and Mudra Therapists are holding the Light in many countries around the world, sharing this knowledge and preserving the accuracy of this ancient technique and proper practice.

This book holds a very special place in my heart. It symbolizes my successfully completed twenty-one year cycle of service to all of you who have read and benefited from my many books. My heart is overflowing with gratitude. May the Universe grant me strength, wisdom and inspiration to be able to serve you the next twenty-one years with equal dedication, enthusiasm and an abundance of joy.

May this book help you manifest your desires and follow your dreams, for it is them that the answer to your life mission hides. Follow your dreams and the Universe will breathe wind into your sails, so you will find the fulfillment you seek. Know in your heart, that Mudras will always help you navigate through your life and successfully find your desired destination. Mudras are our most precious gift, for they belong to us all.

INTRODUCTION

The formidable fusion of Mudras and Crystals initiates a captivating and supernatural experience. Your life is forever transformed and your delicate energy body shifts into an optimal, highly charged state. Of course, to understand and work with these two natural power tools requires your finely tuned participation. Remember, every epiphany in life arrives at the perfectly timed moment, when you are ready to open up and experience something new. Something that will propel your self-realization journey and help fulfill your destiny. Such a metamorphic occurrence will heal, empower and uplift you to become who you truly are, a multi-dimensional being of Light, here to help humanity in our ongoing ascension process.

My dear reader, the moment has come. You are a seeker, a spiritual detective, and a master of your own destiny. Once you've made the conscious decision to embark on the path of self-discovery, you will be gifted with never ending revelations. Here begins a new chapter of your esoteric exploration. You are about to enter the world of finest frequencies and awaken your ability to communicate with Mudras and Crystals. It is a magical world, perhaps much more complex than you expect. And yet, it is absolutely within your reach.

You're on the brink of re-activating an ancient ability that will reveal your life experience in a very different and multi-dimensional way. You are ready to see the unseen, hear the unheard, and feel the energizing effects of deep, well-hidden mysteries. Remember, every event and consequential awakening is a blessing in your life. Sometimes you may not understand this until much later. But when you are ready, a deep sense of recognition will descend upon your inner knowing and then… you've opened another secret gateway.

The portal that you've unlocked at this moment will lead you into a mesmerizing, awe inspiring and otherworldly adventure. Crystals come from mysterious worlds and having close contact and the privilege of their company is profoundly enlightening. You may have had various Crystals for many years and liked them for their decorative value or visual appeal, but in truth, they attracted you for some other, much finer and alchemistic reason. It was their unique frequency, inner light, power and hidden message, that was meant specifically for you.

As I write this book, the world is in a challenging place. However, there has rarely been a time of complete calmness and peace on this planet. Yes, change is constant, unavoidable and unstoppable. The changes of today are exposing us to ongoing EMF radiation, pollution in air, water and food. The health and survival of our planet is at stake. Our communication pathways are instant and as a result, we receive absolutely no opportunity to unwind. We have entered a delicate time of profound frequency level shifts on a grand scale. You are of sensitive nature and have a clear choice; become attuned, resilient and conscious of this shift, or remain lost, increasingly confused and easily swayed into abyss of lower frequencies. Our physical and subtle energy body needs time to rest and regenerate in order to process and clearly absorb new information. If we do not establish this self-healing opportunity, we may fall into a void of sensory numbness, ignorance and eventual gloom.

We need to rely on our natural senses, and avoid getting lost in a maze of misconception. The continuous distractions require determined discipline and stamina in order to maintain a healthy inner balance. Only with clarity of mind, focused effort, open heart and acute awareness will we be able to endure what's ahead.

But have faith, for not all is lost and we are not helpless. To remain self-empowered and become a true anchor for others, you need to know your vulnerabilities. Once you heal them, focus on gaining strength and stamina to move forward and lead the way. Crystals have the unbending power of resilience to withstand any kind of frequency change and will remain solid, unconditional and eager to help you. They can become your most reliable ally and protector. A Crystal can help you heal, recognize and magnify your special gifts and create an impenetrable, resilient energy shield to help withstand any frequency challenge that comes your way. We all have various nonnegotiable obligations and necessities, but no matter what, you always have a choice to find some time for inner reflection and quiet stillness. Developing and cultivating a state of conscious awareness will help you to truly participate in your life.

This book will guide you thru an empowering process of self-discovery, understanding and communication with your Higher Self. In order for this technique to work, you have to be present wholeheartedly and with utmost alertness. It is not enough to collect Crystals for their visual appeal, for you need to know how to work with them properly. When you master this process, the results will be phenomenal.

What is required? Learn to elevate your sensory ability in order to communicate with Crystals. This demands your own subtle body recalibration and proper attunement. For that purpose, you will acquire the very specific technique of working with Mudras and Crystals. The uniquely perfect blending of these two dynamic powers will trigger a profoundly metamorphic effect. Keep in mind, the basic information about Crystals will be explored as far as necessary for our purpose, perhaps in less typical way, but in intricate and never-before-seen partnering alliance of Mudras and Crystals.

My intention is to help you experience a healing growth, strengthen your core, and then access a higher state of consciousness while using Mudras with Crystals to accelerate the process. They compliment and amplify each other in most marvelous ways and I am quite certain your will enjoy this transformative experience. Discover how easily you can conquer challenges, while expanding your perception of our limited reality and ascending beyond the constraints of time and space.

Our Souls are immortal, disappearing and reappearing in this earthly realm only for temporary visits. Their true home is somewhere unseen to human eye. Similarly, Crystals carry gentle yet mighty spirit energies of equally mysterious origins. When these two enigmatic essences dance together, their power blend is an absolutely wondrous pairing.

Mudras and Crystals will help you recognize and accomplish your life mission. With your magnified inner light, you can help make way for others, so that they too may advance on their journey. This is our purpose and our aim. Remember, we are all interconnected.

Thru this Mudra journey, your Crystal will become your loyal, supportive and protective life companion. Crystals are wonderfully reliable and steady. This is what we all need more than we realize. No matter what the situation, steady and solid energy support will help manage your daily challenges.

In this book you will find a wide selection of Mudras and Crystals that will best serve your purpose. Explore which of these suggested Crystals are the best fit for your unique needs and preferences. Take your time and choose them carefully. Your destined Crystals await and you shall find them. We all have various soul contracts we must fulfill, and similarly, your beautiful friends and collaborator Crystals have a mission as well: to help you fulfill your destiny. Together, you can create a perfect pairing, and become the ultimate allies.

Cherish your Crystals and they will appreciate you in return. And if one day, you meet a friend that comes along and seems in need of a true loving companion, listen carefully if one of your Crystals calls out and wants to help your friend in need. At such an occasion, the time has come to part with your Crystal and gift it to your friend. Your Crystal and your friend will be grateful, and you will witness a beginning of a beautiful new friendship. And while you may feel a hint of sadness upon parting, do remember, that your Crystal was never yours. Just like you, every living being is free and belongs only to the Light of the Universe.

Your Crystal companion was here long before you, and will remain here long after you are gone. But these moments in time, and perhaps even a lifetime that you spent together, will transform both of you in a most beautiful way. So enjoy this rare alliance, for every moment of your life is ever changing and fleeting. And the time with your Crystal is one of the most precious, cherished, and unconditionally loving relationships you will ever enjoy. Our lives are an ongoing journey, with a clear purpose to awaken, participate and be fully present.

Now, let's meet our transformative and mighty healing power masters and learn how to work with them properly with the ancient and wondrous Mudras. They have waited for you patiently through the ages, and are eager to share their gifts. Are you ready? Enjoy this adventurous ride and keep beaming your brilliant Light. Live and Love in Light and you shall become the Light…

With Crystal blessings,

Sabrina

Rose Quartz Hearts

Chapter One
About Mudra Alchemy

HOW TO PRACTICE

Mudra for Self ~ Confidence with Amethyst Spheres

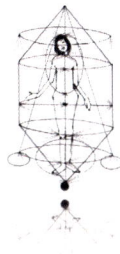

MUDRAS IN ANCIENT TIMES

Mudras originated in ancient Egypt over 5000 years ago and were used by High Priests and Priestesses in sacred healing rituals. Mudras seem quite easy to do, but are immensely powerful and effective when practiced correctly and with precision. There are countless examples of Mudras and hand gestures in iconic figures, sculptures and depictions from all continents of the world. Mudras are truly universal and can be found in every culture on Earth. In addition to advanced work with Mudras and Crystals, the Priests and Priestesses of ancient Egypt used numerous other sensory healing modalities such as advanced healing sound frequencies, color therapy and aromatherapy. I have written about the ancient healing Mudra techniques combined with various modalities in my many Mudra books and online mentorships. However, in this book, I share with you the specific transformative effects of Mudras and Crystals.

WHAT ARE MUDRAS?

Mudras are sacred ancient healing hand gestures that use various intricate positions of fingers, hands, and arms. They carry very specific power activating formulas and can be used with ease, accuracy and assured success. Mudras are clear, simple, yet inexplicably powerful tools for self-healing and empowering your overall physical, mental, and emotional state of well-being while magnifying your spiritual attunement. They are ancient codes to help you recharge, redirect, and reconfigure your subtle energy patterns.

HOW DO MUDRAS WORK?

From an energy anatomy perspective, Mudras work with precision of hand and finger placement. Our fingertips are connected to countless subtle energy currents - Nadis, that affect our entire physical, mental, emotional and energy body. Mudras are very easy to do, and can be practiced by anyone who can move their fingers, arms and hands. Simply by joining your fingertips in specific combinations, you are directly affecting, opening, cleansing, recharging and reactivating your subtle energy currents and Chakra centers. Proper Mudra hand placement is of utmost importance, specifically in relation to your body. A Mudra held above your head will affect you differently than the same Mudra positioned in your lap. Without following these very particular hand - body related placement descriptions, Mudra practice is incomplete and often ineffective. In addition, Mudras have to be practiced with proper breathing techniques to help facilitate and expedite the healing process and the subtle energy movement. Mudras are excellent for unblocking and eliminating congested energy clusters within your subtle body.

AURA, CHAKRAS AND NADIS

Your Aura is a highly perceptive yet invisible subtle energy field and sensory engine that is acutely sensitive to outside stimuli of your immediate environment. Along your spine are seven powerful energy centers, called Chakras. In their optimal state, they are spinning in a clockwise direction. These dynamic vortexes of energy affect every aspect of a specific physical region. They affect your physical health as well as mental and emotional disposition. In addition, your Aura contains 72.000 invisible energy currents called Nadis, running through your body, like subtle energy "veins". They are an intricate part of your highly sophisticated energy field and determine your general state of wellbeing.

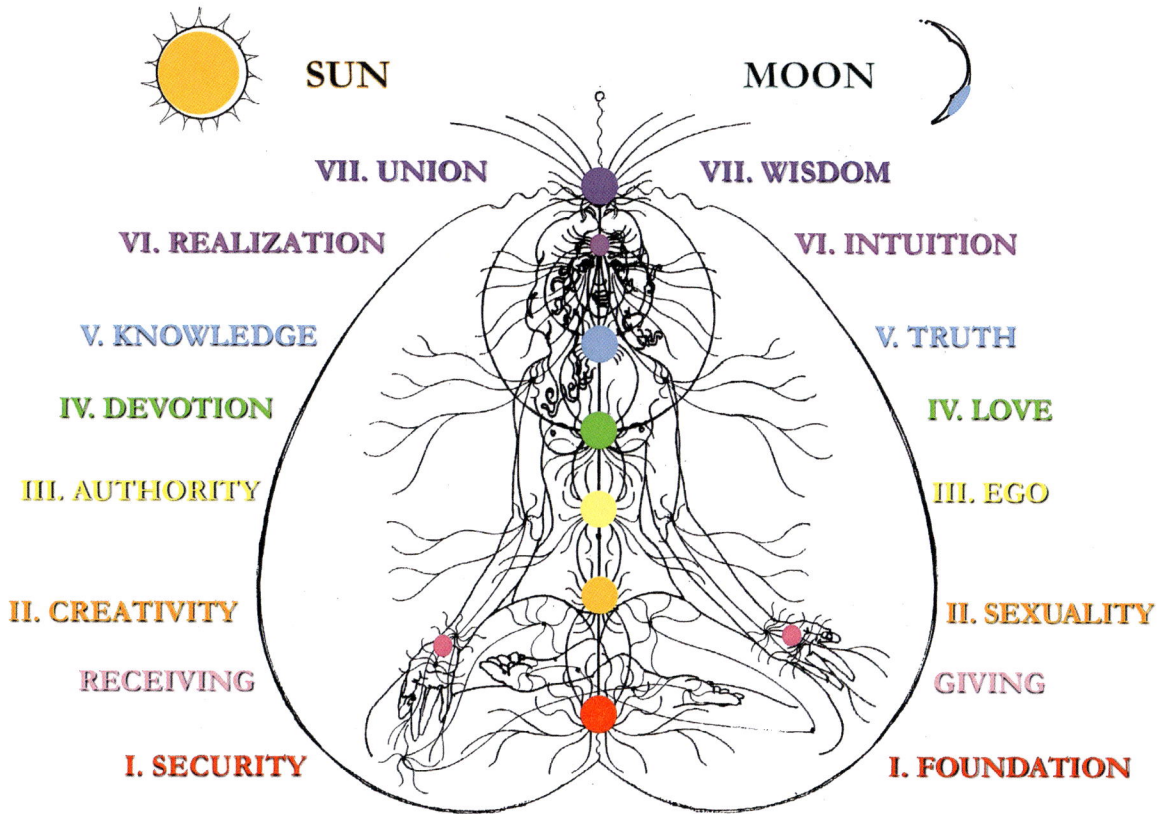

SUN   MOON

VII. UNION   VII. WISDOM

VI. REALIZATION   VI. INTUITION

V. KNOWLEDGE   V. TRUTH

IV. DEVOTION   IV. LOVE

III. AUTHORITY   III. EGO

II. CREATIVITY   II. SEXUALITY

RECEIVING   GIVING

I. SECURITY   I. FOUNDATION

In addition to the seven main Chakra qualities, there are also smaller Chakras in the palms of your hands and soles of your feet. Usually the right hand is on the receiving end of subtle energy, while the left hand is naturally of more giving nature, since it is closer to your heart. The right side of your body is under the influence of the Sun, while the left side is under the influence of the Moon. As a result, the right hand affects one's mental and logical perception and is reflection of your masculine nature, while the left hand expresses your intuitive, emotional, feminine side. This placement is part of each person's subtle energy field. The ability of giving and receiving subtle energy can vary depending on the individual. A highly sensory aware and intuitive person may be able to use both hands for intentional subtle energy transmitting, sharing, scanning , reading, healing, as well as receiving.

HEALING BREATH

Another very important aspect of Mudra practice is proper breathing. It has an immediate connection to your emotional state. You breathe differently when you are tired, stressed, pessimistic or when you are excited, happy and peaceful. When practicing controlled breathing, you will immediately calm down and center your entire being. During the Mudra practice, the inhalation and exhalation should always be practiced thru the nose and centered at the solar plexus region. Place both palms of your hands on your stomach area and feel it expand with each inhalation and contract with each exhalation. Mudras are most often practiced in a slow, long and deep breathing rhythm.

Occasionally when so noted, you may use the fast, short breath of fire, which works under the same principles, but at a faster pace. With the breath of fire, the focus is on a more forceful exhalation, generated with a strong contracting movement of your stomach muscle. Always use your own judgment and remain comfortable during your Mudra practice. If needed, return back to the long, deep breathing to complete the recommended three-minute Mudra exercise. Remember, your breath holds the delicate balance between your physical body and your Soul. It keeps you alive, connected and present in this world and impacts every second of your life.

POSTURE & EYES

The proper posture during Mudra practice is essential. A comfortable position with a straight back will allow all your subtle energy centers - Chakras and Nadis, to open up and function at their best capacity. Your shoulders should be in a fixed position and must not move during your breathing. The only motion is the expanding and contracting of your rib cage, accompanying each breath. During the Mudra practice, it is best to close your eyes, and gently direct the gaze towards the Third eye center. You can also keep them half open and lightly look over the tip of your nose. You may look into the middle far away distance and relax the eyelids. Never force your fingers, hands, body or your eyes into a painful or uncomfortable position.

MEDITATION

During and after your Mudra practice, you will find yourself in deep meditation. It will fell natural to remain still, and enjoy the elevated state of consciousness. It is most beneficial to take advantage of this most receptive and potent self-healing state. Continue with your long, deep breathing and allow you mind to settle into a most peaceful and serene demeanor of complete stillness. There are many types of meditation and you can use Mudras in combination with various meditation techniques. I suggest you do not preoccupy yourself with what you are supposed to experience, but simply allow the natural process to override any restless inner dialogue. Meditation is essential for cultivating your daily inner calm and will greatly help you overcome various challenging situations. Approaching life with tranquility and a deep connection with the Divine will assist you in leading a happier and healthier life.

CONCENTRATION

Firmly hold your mind on a specific desired topic and direct your closed eyes towards your Third Eye area. Gently look slightly upward and direct your gaze far into the distance. That is your focus point where you can penetrate through the limited perception and glimpse into the higher realm of infinity. If you need an answer to a specific question, inquire your Higher consciousness. Only a clear question can receive a clear answer. Do not overanalyze. If you receive no answer, let go, and know that in due time your question will be answered.

VISUALIZATION

Your mind is an extremely powerful instrument. With the practice of Mudras and meditation you will learn to bring your mind into a state of absolute stillness and focus. You can practice visualization to help envision a healthy state of your body, a serendipitous circumstance, or a favorable outcome of an event. By visualizing a calming and healing environment, you can transform your well-being, reduce stress, and improve your overall health.

Visualization is equally important when you desire to attract love and abundance. Seeing yourself successful in your mind will attract circumstances and people who will help you succeed. Visualization is very easy and can be practiced anywhere. Mudra practice is an excellent opportunity to visualize the desired outcome. For example, when practicing the Mudra for Protecting your Health, visualize your body surrounded by vibrant restorative energy, filling your with brightest healing light. Create a powerful sphere where you can manifest your aspirations.

AFFIRMATIONS

During the Mudra practice your mind becomes receptive and open to positive input. This is an excellent time to consciously establish a positive inner dialogue, and use an affirmation of your choice. You may say the affirmation out loud before or after the Mudra practice, or repeat it in your mind during the entire exercise. Affirmations are always practiced with an openness that allows the Universe to bring about your wish, while you make an honest effort to help this become a reality. However, once you have done your part, allow the Universe to manifest the fulfillment of your desire in whatever way is best for you, and the higher good of all. Chose affirmations in a most positive sense and avoid using any negative words. Affirm a positive outcome, a happy joyful state, optimal health and general optimism about your life. Repeat every word with true conviction, reflect on the meaning of it, while consciously embedding it into your mindset so that it becomes part of your healthy belief system and thinking pattern. A most powerful affirmation is your expression of gratitude. It carries wide reaching positive effects on all of your life circumstances. No matter how dire your situation, if you insist on finding elements you are grateful for, your effort will quickly overpower negative thought patterns in your mind. Your gratitude will attract positive and new energy into all areas of your life.

HOW LONG SHOULD YOU PRACTICE?

Each Mudra needs to be practiced at least three minutes. Allow two additional minutes for sitting in stillness and meditation. As little as this may seem, do not underestimate the power of Mudras. When you develop a regular practice you will feel the positive effects faster and stronger. A longer practice option is eleven minutes for each Mudra. You may practice as many Mudras as you wish. A combined thirty-minute daily Mudra and following meditation practice is an excellent and most beneficial routine. Ideal practice time is in the morning or before going to sleep at night.

MUDRAS, MANTRAS AND CRYSTALS

Mantras add a deeply transformative power of healing sound vibrations to your Mudra practice. Mantras resonate within your body in a most potent way. The hard palate in your mouth has fifty-eight power points that connect to your subtle body's energy meridians and affect your entire being. By singing, speaking, or whispering mantras, you are activating these energy points in a specific order and pattern that has a harmonious and healing effect on your physical, mental, emotional and spiritual body. The sound frequency resonates with each chakra and each cell of your body. The ancient science of mantras thus helps you reactivate and properly realign your chakras and nadis. In addition, mantras magnify your concentration, and are profoundly effective in stilling your mind. For example, when singing OM, you are affecting your entire body beginning at the First and ending at the Seventh Chakra. For a clear demonstration of the harmonious effect of sound on your body, take a long, deep breath and slowly sing A-E-I-O-U-M.

Feel the sound as it travels from your lower spine and ends with powerful vibration of MMM in your forehead. The healing frequency of this sound realigns your entire body. Combining mantra and Mudra practice facilitates an experience of multidimensional healing. When you add Crystals to this practice, your own naturally produced healing sound frequency is further magnified by the healing and energizing effects of the Crystals. This technique activates your extra sensory abilities to help you recognize and work with the finest subtle frequencies that we obviously can't easily see or hear. But your mantra sound frequency is registered and positively magnified by your Crystal collaborator. As you sing Mantras that apply to each Mudra, consciously perceive the frequency of your own voice, traveling from your throat towards the Crystal and back. Feel the harmonious resonance escalate and charge you with vital life force. As you deepen and advance your practice, the experience will magnify and you will feel the Crystal vibrate, as if it were singing along with your voice. It is a beautiful duet that harmonizes your resonance and propels your ascent towards the Light.

Your Hands and the Cosmos

In addition to revitalizing your entire energy body, Mudras offer impressive benefits to accelerate your mental abilities, balance your emotions and elevate your state of consciousness. This specific effects occur when selected fingers are joined or kept apart, hands and palms turned in various directions, and each Mudra placed correctly in relation to your body. As I mentioned previously, Mudras are not isolated gestures, disconnected from your body's physical posture. All details such as the height and direction of the pointed fingers and palms are of the greatest importance, especially when your aim is to eliminate a challenging mental obstacle or increase a desired ability, improve a weakened state or develop and activate special gifts.

Our physical body also experiences a fascinating impact of the solar system. The right side of the body is ruled by the Sun, the male and mental aspect, and the left side is under the influence of the Moon, expressing your feminine, emotional energy. Furthermore, each finger relates to a specific planet, creating intricate network of interconnected triggers in your disposition, strengths, weaknesses, challenges as well as special abilities and gifts. This is one of the reasons why it is of significant importance which fingers connect and which hand is on top of the other, as well as where they are held in relation to your body.

Thumb ~ MARS - God, willpower, logic, ego

Index ~ JUPITER - knowledge, wisdom, self-confidence

Middle finger ~ SATURN - patience, emotional control

Ring finger ~ SUN - love, health, vitality, life energy

Little finger ~ MERCURY - communication, creativity, beauty

PLANETARY INFLUENCE ON YOUR FINGERS

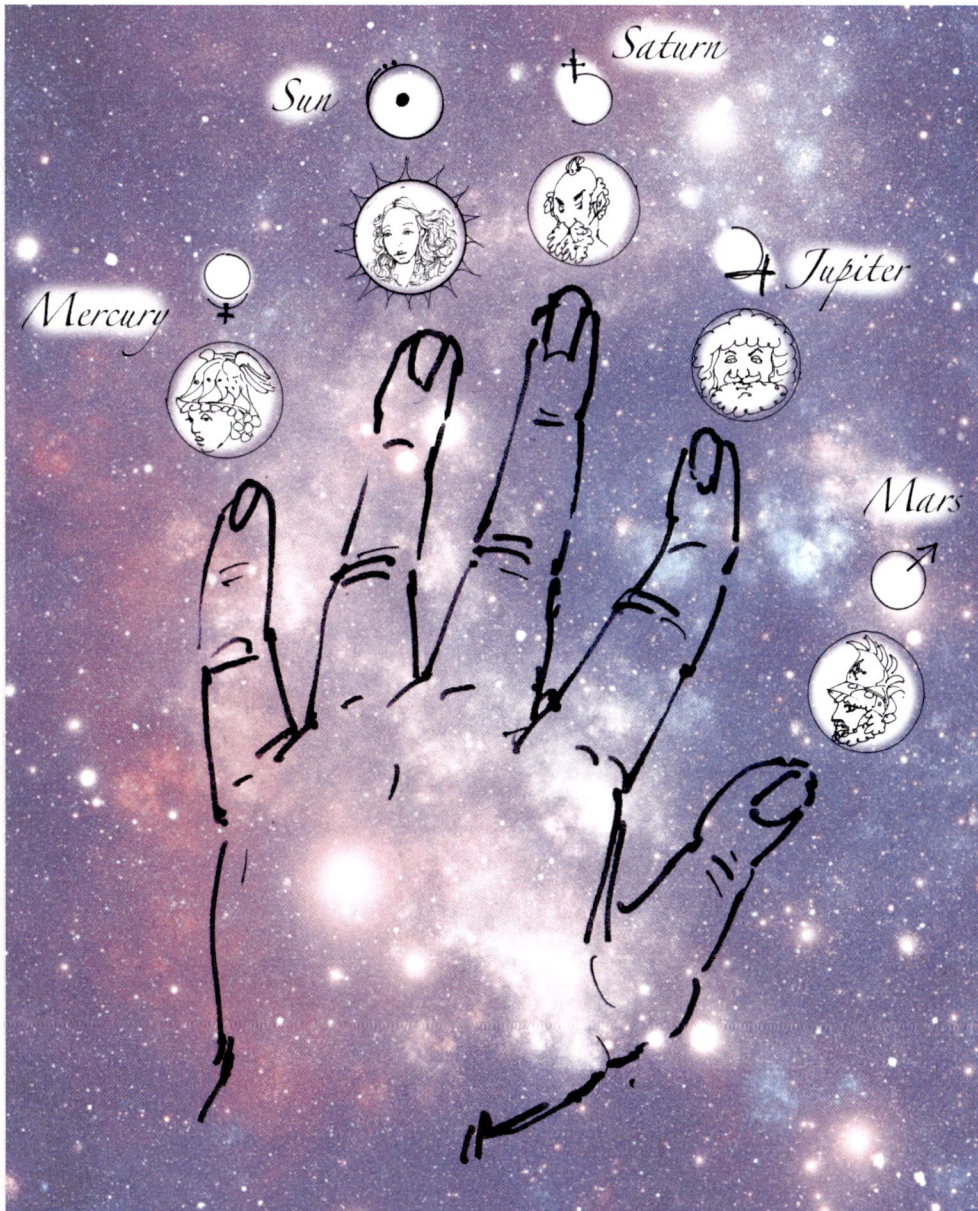

**MUDRAS ARE YOUR ANCIENT KEYS
TO UNLOCK THE MAGNIFICENT POWER WITHIN.**

**ALL THE ANSWERS YOU ARE SEEKING
ARE IN YOUR OWN HANDS.**

BENEFITS OF YOUR MUDRA PRACTICE

Emotional and mental states continuously transform and shape your energy body in response to environment, other people and events that occur in your life. You may have a mentally, emotionally or spiritually challenging day, which won't necessarily display in your physical appearance, however your subtle energy body will absorb the disruptive energy and you will feel the consequences. Likewise, you could be going through an emotionally stressful situation, which won't visibly affect your physical body, but will definitely affect your energy body. If these dynamics continue, your physical body will eventually display dis-ease as a result of long-term stressors on finer energy levels. You won't be able to keep up the facade forever. If your everyday challenges are considerable, your subtle energy body will need to compromise as well as substitute for your energy depletion. Proper practice of Mudras will help release negative energy, limit the onset of disease and promote a healthy overall functioning. The beneficial effects will magnify with regular practice.

Mudras work on the finer, subtler energy levels that are invisible to the human eye. As a result, the benefits of Mudra practice are multi layered and reach far beyond simple physical improvements.

DURING MUDRA PRACTICE, YOU ARE CONNECTING THE ENERGY CURRENTS FROM TWO OPPOSITE POLES OF THE RIGHT AND LEFT SIDE OF YOUR BODY. THIS CREATES AN ENERGY SURGE, OPENS UP BLOCKED NADIS AND INCREASES VITAL ENERGY FLOW FOR REGENERATION AND VITALITY.

In complex cases with long term challenging emotional, physical or mental issues, we need to apply Mudra Therapy™ principles, which I describe in my book **MUDRA THERAPY**, *Hand Yoga for Pain Management and Conquering Ilness.*

At the core of any self-improvement or self-help healing modality is the need for proper evaluation about the source and deeper nature of your challenge. Simply using the *Mudra for help with Stress* will help temporarily, but will be less effective for a long term solution, unless we eliminate the source of stress and disengage in stressful situations or dynamics. Finding and eliminating the source of stress is the crucial and deciding factor. Similarly, *Mudra for a Healthy Diet* won't do you any good, if you continue to indulge in unhealthy eating patterns. In short, there is no escaping the need to find and address the core issue of your challenge. Once that is established, you can apply Mudras that will help you overcome, reprogram and discontinue unhealthy behavior and replace it with new and healthy habits.

Finally, the countless Mudra benefits are magnified when properly practiced with energy generators and magnifiers - our Crystal friends. The combination of these two power tools is uniquely beneficial on the physical, mental and emotional levels as well as on your delicate, subtler energy fields.

Chapter Two
About Crystal Alchemy

BEINGS OF LIGHT

Mudra for Creative Guidance with tumbled Stones

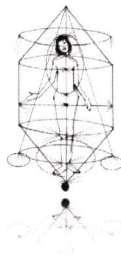

THE ORIGINS AND HISTORY OF CRYSTALS

The first use of Crystals dates back to the time of ancient Egypt, over 5000 years ago. However, it is important to acknowledge a theory about two other civilizations that used Crystals in a significant way. These were the ancient civilization of Lemuria and Atlantis. They are believed to have both ended in absolute destruction on a large scale, when possibly hit by devastating natural disasters. And while Lemuria is considered more of a scientific hypothesis, the story of Atlantis dates back to Plato, who spend many years studying in ancient Egypt. He described Atlantis as a peaceful land in the middle of Atlantic ocean, and even though some historians regard this as fiction, similar information can be found in Egyptian records. There are numerous indications about the highly evolved Atlantis civilization, their abilities for telepathic communication, the loving and paradise-like atmosphere, and most of all, their supremely advanced knowledge and use of Crystals. Plato described how eventually this very evolved civilization took a dark turn when the inhabitants unfortunately succumbed to greed and ignorance of divine laws. Atlantis quickly fell into a state of doom and deteriorated from a peaceful nation to a self-destructive one. Shortly thereafter it suffered a catastrophic flood and rapidly sank into the ocean. The Atlantis civilization perished and to this day there are endless attempts to uncover the real truth about its existence.

Why is this of interest to us? In regards to use of Crystals, some writings state that in Atlantean as well as Lemurian highly evolved culture of telepathic communication, a very sophisticated and advanced technique was used to embed their most valuable and treasured information and ancient wisdom into specially selected Crystals. When faced with the unavoidable downfall and utter destruction, the ancient Wise-ones and Light-workers that carefully guarded the advanced Crystal technology, attempted to preserve, protect and hide it in a very specific way - with a complex embedding process. Upon completion of their preservation efforts, they rematerialized the Crystals into the Earth for safe keeping. The purpose was to somehow leave this highly valuable information for surviving and future civilizations. To this day, many dedicated Crystal studies mention these rare Crystals that contain the ancient information. We can study and learn from them, at least in our limited capacity. These Crystals are called Lemurian Star Seed Crystals and Record Keepers from Atlantis.

Lemurian Star Seed Quartz

ANCIENT EGYPT

According to ancient Egyptian and astrophysicist theories, it was possibly the preserved knowledge from Atlantis that helped create the advanced culture of Egypt. Were they able to build their impressive majestic pyramids with such mysterious ease because of some supremely advanced technique? Were they following the principles of the Atlantean pyramids? There are numerous ancient pyramids in Central America, China, Europe and throughout the world, that could be further examples of the advanced technology and knowledge passed down from the embedded Crystals of Lemuria and Atlantis. Whoever and whatever the source that accomplished such seemingly impossible feats is, there is one aspect that is particularly interesting.

The pyramid's perfect geometry is patterned after the structure of Crystal principles of physics. As a result, it has the powerful ability to emit as well as channel high frequency vibrations. These frequencies are able to reach further than imaginable and can "communicate" in ways utterly inconceivable to us. There are other descriptions of Crystal use in ancient Egyptian times, in connection with the pyramids and their powerful presence and purpose. The pyramid building blocks consist of limestone and granite, with the latter containing about 25% quartz. The ancient Egyptian sarcophagi were usually also made of granite and therefore likewise contained high levels of Crystals. Some pyramids had their entire uppermost piece, called *pyramidion*, enclosed with an enormous Crystal, glowing and emitting the highest of frequencies. It seems that one of the pyramid's purposes was to generate, balance and harmonize energy in a very wide geographical area. Another very possible intention may have been to facilitate highly advanced communication with faraway star systems. This brings us to the widely known conclusion that the pyramids of ancient Egypt were never used as tombs, but rather as immense power generators.

The Crystal structure itself retains the power of an unwavering frequency. When you work with Mudras and these ancient and highly intelligent Crystal being, the forces connecting with your individual life force are capable of magnificent metamorphic accomplishments.

Carnelian

CRYSTAL HEALING IN ANCIENT TIMES

Crystals were used worldwide throughout the ages, mostly for countless healing purposes such as diagnosing illness, and evoking energy protection in Mayan, Native American, and Indian cultures. For the intention of our Mudra and Crystal practice, ancient Egypt is of the highest interest to us. It is important to note, that Crystals were used in combination with numerous other advanced sensory healing modalities, such as healing sound frequency, aromatherapy and color therapy. The latter remains to this day considerably under-developed, almost dormant, or is used only in very basic ways.

In ancient Egypt, Crystals of specific colors were placed in various window-like openings of selected structures, usually at highly powerful predetermined architectural points. The purpose was to activate them during very particular and auspicious dates, when planetary configurations and transits facilitated a powerful energy shift. When the sunlight or moonlight pierced directly through the carefully positioned Crystals, a highly charged healing color beam would project onto all participants during sacred initiating ceremonies. This occurred most often at times of summer or winter Solstice, at sunrise and sunset, as well as at night in connection to various Moon transit and eclipse ceremonies.

There is much evidence of healing Crystals highly valued and revered status in ancient Egypt. Looking at the very precise and intentional use of Crystals in their ritual ornaments as well as funeral traditions, it is quite obvious that the ancient Egyptians were supremely aware and knowledgeable of various Crystal qualities, benefits and transformative healing powers. Additionally, Crystals were used in healing and advanced medical procedures, transmitting and evoking high vibrational healing frequencies in health emergencies and during intricate surgeries. In ancient Egyptology research documents, there have been notations and discoveries of highly advanced precise Crystal remedy formulas used on patients that suffered from life threatening injuries or illnesses. With their higher and deeper understanding of Crystal healing powers, Egyptians often crushed the Crystals into powder form and used them in liquid medicinal dosages. The intention was to ease and expedite the absorption process and help recalibrate the depleted frequency of the patient's physical body. With the help of high frequency Crystal potions, higher frequency quickly permeated the patient's body, and effectively healed the diseased and energetically depleted physical organs or body parts. With this advanced techniques of tapping into the unwavering and indestructible Crystal frequency stabilizers, an overall higher level of cellular harmony was quickly and successfully re-established in the patient.

INTUITION AND PROTECTION

In ancient Egypt, Crystals we also extensively used to specifically evoke and magnify intuition, and establish protective subtle energy shields. The color of gems was of high importance. One of the most prized stones Lapis Lazuli which comes in beautiful shades of blue, symbolized the heavens. King Tutankhamen's golden mask shows the extensive use of Lapis around the eyes. Lapis is a high vibration stone and positively affects the Third Eye Center while empowering one's intuitive ability. Similarly, very specialized and definitive stones were used in funeral and afterlife preparation, as well as generously supplied in and around the sarcophagus. The sarcophagus of King Tutankhamen was made of yellow quartzite, a crystalline rock with over 90% quartz Crystal.

CRYSTAL STRUCTURE

It is actually not clear how long it takes for Crystals to form, it could certainly be thousands of years or they could manifest and emerge almost instantaneously. What is absolutely fascinating is the fact that Crystal structures are composed in very specific formations of subtle vibrations that resonate in perfect harmony with cosmic frequency. The Crystal molecules are arranged in a very symmetrical pattern that facilitates their exceptionally stable, consistent and extremely potent frequency.

WHERE CAN YOU FIND CRYSTALS

You can find mineral deposits of Crystals in rich veins of the Earth. These are slightly open spaces where minerals are crystalized. Some of these Crystals can be retrieved with a simple chisel and hammer, while larger Crystal chambers need to be blasted open. Another place to find Crystals is in natural streams. The fine gravel at the bottom of a stream needs to be shaken and cleaned under water in order to separate and find natural Crystals. One of the world's best known Crystals caves was discovered in Mexico, while digging a new tunnel in a mine, at the depth of 890 feet below surface. The Crystals in the cave were extremely large, up to thirty-nine feet in length and thirteen feet in diameter. The cave environment was very challenging and extremely hot at 136 Fahrenheit with 99% humidity. The cave interior was extensively researched and filmed and the documentation is quite stunning and very informative. As of 2017 the caves have re-flooded and remain inaccessible.

CRYSTAL USE IN TODAY'S TECHNOLOGY

Quartz Crystal can transform energy from one form to another. The material properties of quartz Crystal are extremely resilient, stable and can withstand time, temperature, and other environmental changes. It is for this unique reason that Crystals are ideal for use in numerous applications such as smartphones, computers, digital cameras, clocks, vehicles, radios, audio players, car navigation systems, medical equipment, robotics and a vast range of other electronics. In the old days, one could create a very simple version of a radio with bare minimum components, and one of them is a Crystal. They are undoubtedly an important, intricate, and definitely irreplaceable part of our technology today, and will remain so in the foreseeable future.

Lapis

HOW DO CRYSTALS WORK?

Crystal structure aligns itself with the Universal cosmic force and creates a very purified clear form of matter. This physical manifestation vibrates in perfect harmony with its originating Universal energy. The actual point of the Crystal form aligns each tiniest part of it with the infinite cosmic energy. To the contrary of the perfect unison in Crystal formation, our bodies are built of various kinds of molecules that radiate at different frequencies and electrical charge. Therefore it is a considerable challenge for us to establish a completely harmonious overall pattern and maintain a balanced state throughout our many layers of physical, mental, emotional and finer energy bodies.

THE EFFECTS OF CRYSTALS ON YOUR ENERGY BODY

Crystals increase the light force in your aura and stimulate your finer energy bodies. They act as mighty powerful generators. When you hold a Crystal in your hands, you are instantly in touch with the forces that shaped our planet and the elements that first formed, eons ago in the distant stars of our galaxy. The Crystals are catalysts for integration of more color, light and energy into your many energy centers. In addition, the increased frequency has the power to dissipate and diminish any dark clusters of negative energy and unseen blockages that you carry. The undesirable or weak energy that you may not even be aware of, can be transformed into clean, recharged and easily flowing energy, all with the help of Crystal. As a result, Crystals can be used for your subtle body healing as well as a protective shield from negative frequencies. A Crystal helps clear, advance and protect unobstructed functioning and positive state of all your subtle energy bodies, as well as physical body, mind and spirit. Crystals simply help you shine.

CRYSTALS CAN RECEIVE, HOLD, BEAM, BEND AND MIRROR LIGHT. LIGHT IS THE SUPREME ENERGY OF OUR PHYSICAL UNIVERSE. CRYSTALS HAVE THE CAPACITY TO OPEN THE GATEWAYS TO HIGHER DIMENSIONS.

WHY ARE CRYSTALS SO SPECIAL?

When you master the deeper understanding of Crystal essence, you gain a special privilege - access to their immense wisdom. A communication channel is established that enables you to clearly receive and understand their personal messages to you. Yes, Crystals seem to be motionless, but in fact they move large energy mass in a most effective, seemingly invisible ways. This is something that may sound highly unusual. Open your mind to the possibility that you are actually able to receive communication that doesn't come from another human, or an animal, but from an entirely different perfect high frequency being - a Crystal. And if this sounds a bit unreal, it is time to expand your limited perception. Superior communication can occur in any form of frequency. All that is required is your open receptivity and a naturally heightened personal frequency. In other words, it is like a finely tuned version of reliably intuitive telepathy, activated at will.

WHEN YOUR INDIVIDUAL FREQUENCY VIBRATES WITHOUT DISRUPTIONS, YOU CAN ASCEND TO THE LEVEL OF UNDERSTANDING AND ENGAGING IN PURE FREQUENCY COMMUNICATION.

EXPANDING YOUR CONCEPT OF FRIENDS AND GUIDES

Obviously you and I are human and we relate to friends in a limited way - only as other humans. However, let's not dismiss our pets as most loyal life-long friends. Why not also consider plants as our helpful and soothing friends of a different kind? It is essential for your evolutionary progress to expand your perception and understand that friends, guides and protectors come in many shapes and forms. Especially since our recognition and ability of finer subtle energies is so limited. If you think about the most important, valuable and irreplaceable qualities of a true ally, you may come up with a list that no human can fulfill. The one dependable source that will always have the right answer and solutions to your questions and challenges is your Higher Consciousness. If a friend can be your "mirror", it will always help you find the answers you are seeking for and already know deep in your Soul. A Crystal can be your most unusual "friend", very reliable in its stabile and unwavering subtle energy support.

A CRYSTAL ACTS AS A MIRROR AND A RELIABLE COUNTERPART WHILE RAISING YOUR FREQUENCY.

IT HELPS YOU ACCESS YOUR HIGHER CONSCIOUSNESS SO THAT YOU ARE CLEAR, EMPOWERED AND INDEPENDENT.

IN THIS CONTEXT, A CRYSTAL IS YOUR SUPPORTIVE, OBJECTIVE AND RELIABLE FRIEND, COLLABORATOR, PROTECTOR AND ALLY.

Green Zebra Jasper

THE POWER OF QUARTZ CRYSTALS

This powerful clear Crystal works on multidimensional levels of being. It vibrates clear white light, which contains all other colors. It generates electromagnetism and has the ability to magnify, absorb, store, release, and regulate energy. When you hold a Quartz Crystal in your hand it doubles your bio-magnetic aura field, and can take your energy level to the optimal state possible, the way it was before any disease or disharmony settled in your system.

THE QUARTZ IS A MIGHTY SOUL CLEANSER AND COSMIC BEAM. IT HOLDS ANCIENT INFORMATION THAT CAN GREATLY ENHANCE YOUR METAPHYSICAL ABILITIES.

IN A DEEPER SPIRITUAL SENSE, THE QUARTZ CAN HELP YOU DISSOLVE ANY UNWANTED KARMIC SEEDS AND FIND YOUR SPIRITUAL PURPOSE .

Quartz is found in many shapes and formations which have specific and unique properties. It has six sides which symbolize the six chakras. The termination of the Crystal - the point - is the crown chakra, connecting you with the Universal power, the infinite wisdom. Crystals often have a flat base which was originally their root. Sometimes Quartz has a certain cloudiness at the bottom which clears as you approach the point, symbolizing our own clarity when we elevate our consciousness. Because Quartz radiates the divine light, by seeing, holding, and meditating with it, you can work with bringing the Light into physical form.

Whatever Crystals you attract into your life will be helpful with your growing process. If a person is not aware of the powerful healing energy of the Crystal, the positive effects will be working in a subliminal way. But if you are aware of the higher frequency within the Crystal, it will become your greatest tool and ally, helping you beam the Light into your life and this world.

Crystals work like pyramids, channeling high frequency onto this Earth plane while stimulating the finer frequencies. Each Crystal has a unique character and identity, stemming from its particular and long life experiences. One of the rare qualities is the ability to vibrate its energy at all color frequencies, demonstrating how to manifest the purity of white light into lower frequencies. This unique capacity can help teach us how to activate our own power to vibrate all our chakras simultaneously in perfect alignment. This is usually one of our main challenges of living in this physical form.

Quartz has the intelligence to merge the Light force with the physical plane elements, which facilitates our healing process. Gradually we can learn to vibrate in perfect harmony. Quartz Crystals can vibrate the human aura at such a high frequency rate, that it dissolves and releases the darker tones of our karmic seeds.

Clear quartz Crystals sometimes resemble entire galaxies, which demonstrates that worlds exist within worlds. This might be challenging to understand within our limited mind capacity. However, Crystals teach us to open up and grasp more complex concepts, while elevating us onto a higher frequency. As a result, our ability to discern can expand beyond our limitations.

Some Crystals carry with them unique markings, records and information, and often change thru the years, sometimes completely clearing the cloudiness inside. The lists of various Crystal formations and types is truly endless. There are however a few most fascinating kinds that we'll explore a little closer. Keep in mind that some Crystals have been polished to enhance their natural hidden beauty. However, natural Crystals that have not been altered are quite breathtaking. A Crystal does not lose its frequency when polished, a perfect example is a Crystal sphere. It is a powerful tool to see beyond and into the never-ending possibilities of your future.

Rainbow Quartz

Bridge Quartz

Herkimer Diamond

Bridge & Barnacle Quartz

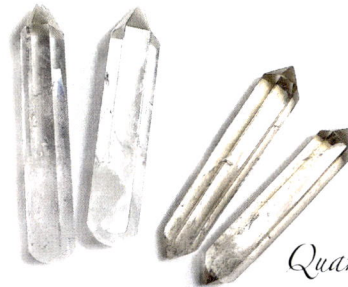

Quartz Wands

Quartz Cluster

Abundance Extended Quartz

Quartz Crystal Agents of Change

Herkimer Diamond Crystal
A small, yet the most powerful of all quartz Crystals.
It transmits and receives spiritual energy, is very transparent,
and double terminated. It is like a mini dynamo.
This is a high vibration stone.

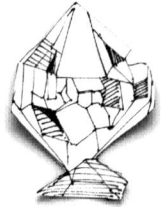

Abundance Crystal
Crystal points with smaller Crystals growing around its base.
They help attract and create abundance.

Cross Crystal
Crossing Crystal is joined to the other, but does
not completely penetrate it. Ideal for equality, unity,
harmony, understanding and acceptance.

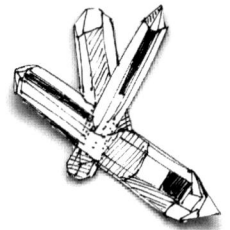

Bridge Crystal
A smaller Crystal growing out of another at nearly right angle
with the base of the smaller Crystal inside the larger one.
Most of the smaller Crystal is outside of the larger one.
It facilitates a move from the spirit world
to the physical one.

Inner Child Crystal
Similar to a bridge Crystal, in which a small Crystal
is growing out of a much larger one, but in this case
only a small amount of it is extruding. It teaches you
acceptance of your past and present.

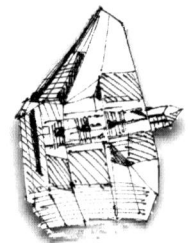

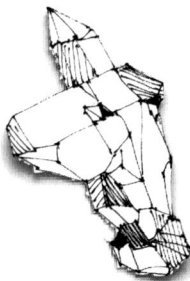

Double Terminated Crystal
A powerful Crystal containing two distinct
terminations and no base.
A great receiver and transmitter
to the higher planes.

RECORD KEEPER CRYSTAL - ATLANTIS

This Crystal has fascinating and clearly etched pyramid
shapes on its termination faces. It is very rare.
It holds the ancient wisdom of the Wise Ones from
the times of Atlantis. These Crystals are often invisible
or hidden and revealed only when the right person finds them.

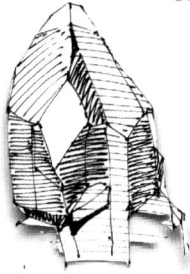

DIAMOND WINDOW CRYSTAL

Clearly visible four-sided vertical diamond shaped
"window" as one of the six main faces. Very special.
A window to see yourself and receive information
you may need at this very moment.

LEMURIAN SEED CRYSTAL

This Master Crystal displays horizontal pattern
of coded grooves on one or more sides.
This is a rare Crystal that can be used in many
applications as well as spiritual healings
to help reestablish overall balance within.
Great precision is needed when
working with this Crystal.

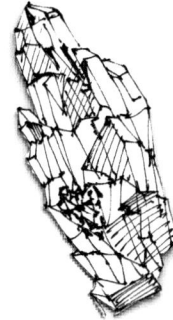

TIME LINE TO FUTURE CRYSTAL

Contains a seventh parallelogram Activation Window,
that is just below the six main faces of the termination,
at an angle leaning right. It is very helpful in focusing
your actions on a specific desired future state.

TIME LINE TO PAST CRYSTAL

This Crystal has a seventh face that is just below the
six main faces of the termination, leaning to the left.
It will help you gain a deeper understanding of your past
and how it relates to your issues today.

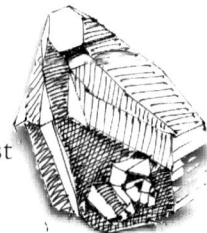

PHANTOM CRYSTAL

A fascinating Crystal that contains a ghost-like
image of another Crystal within it, that is
harmoniously aligned with the outer Crystal.
It assists you to get in touch with your inner self.

RAINBOW CRYSTAL

An unusual Crystal that contains internal crack
formations which display a marvelous rainbow
when viewed from an angle. It assist in
healing grief, despair, loss, or pain.

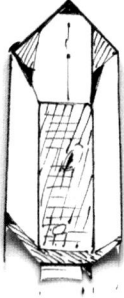

GENERATOR CRYSTAL

A single Crystal with six sharp facets meeting in a sharp point.
It has the ability to gather the Universal life force
and hold it in its sacred depository. This is a superior Crystal,
ideal for amplifying energy and focus, and is
a dynamic power source for other Crystals.

LASER CRYSTAL

A striking, naturally formed long and slender Crystal
that tapers towards termination. Whenever you hold this laser wand,
the healing energy will surround your body, and secure
a protective barrier. Excellent for use in a healing process
that requires a powerful energy shift.

TEACHER CRYSTAL

This kind of Crystal is very personal and can have any form.
It can be identified in course of time, through deep connection.
When you realize that your perception and knowledge is expanding
faster than ever, you have found your Teacher.
Don't ever let it go, or allow it to be touched or used
by anyone else but you. It is a divinely personal Crystal.

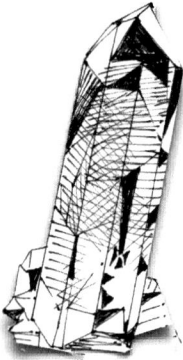

MANIFESTATION CRYSTAL

This rare Crystal contains another visible Crystal within.
It magnifies your ability to see the world with profoundly
optimistic, almost childlike joy and enthusiasm.

LARGE EARTH KEEPER CRYSTAL

This Crystal is a manifestation of massive power and intellect, containing
supreme information about time, our physical plane of existence,
the highest principles of truth and unconditional love.
It holds an intricate power point in our
Earth subtle energy grid and helps sustain
delicate balance between invisible dimensions.
It is physically a very large Crystal body.

Chapter Three
The Alchemy of You
YOUR SUBTLE ENERGY LAYERS

Mudra for Powerful Insight with Pyrite~Fool's Gold

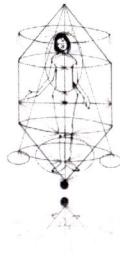

Your Mission

Now that we met the two important contributors to our healing journey, let's not forget about the main participant. And that my dear, is YOU. Yes, all the wonderful benefits that Mudra technique offers and amazing frequency boosts that Crystals create, can't really make a difference without your attentive participation. You are the one who has to consciously prepare to facilitate this intricate subtle energy collaboration.

What is required of you? Time, effort and a clear intention, mixed with a pure desire to grow and learn. It requires more than just reading about this process. It actually demands for your deeper reflection, soul searching and honest examination of your habits, tendencies, fears, and all hidden dynamics that are in your way. This could entail an unhealthy physical condition, a challenging mental disposition or remains of an emotional upheaval from your past that you still carry within your very own frequency and subtle energy field. Wherever you feel a general sense of unease, conflict, stress and challenge, that is where your inner work is required.

The moment you embark on this journey of self-discovery, you will begin to uncover the many important details that matter and contribute to your current situation in life. We are in this world to learn, make progress, ascend and be of service. Once you consciously recognize this concept, you are on your way.

For the purpose of working with this book in a most systematic way, I suggest you get yourself a small notebook. Before you practice Mudras and Crystal sets, write down all your questions, thoughts and concerns. After your practice, notate your reflections and any clear revelations that may have come your way. Accessing your higher consciousness on demand requires regular practice. It is like a muscle that needs stretching and strengthening. These are the necessary stepping stones that are an important part of your journey.

Our mission is to help you clear energy obstacles and challenges and strengthen your Aura - subtle energy field. This will result in crisp focus and clarity about who you are, and what are your goals. Your intentions may shift and evolve as you progress. Once you understand how to manage and consciously clear your energy field, you will be able to create and sustain an invisible energy shield of protection. This will help keep you untouchable to any disruptive energies, frequencies and negative forces that may come your way.

**THE ABILITY TO SEAL OFF YOUR PERSONAL AURA FIELD
IS OF EXISTENTIAL NATURE AND WILL HELP PROTECT AND PRESERVE
YOUR PHYSICAL, MENTAL AND EMOTIONAL HEALTH.**

THIS IS BEYOND IMPORTANT, IT IS URGENT AND IMPERATIVE.

**IN TODAY'S CHALLENGING AND ADVERSE FREQUENCY ENVIRONMENT,
THE RESILIENCE OF YOUR OWN SUBTLE ENERGY FIELD IS PARAMOUNT.**

BUILDING YOUR INNER AWARENESS

Usually, the most popular way to use Crystals is in simple meditations while holding or sitting with them, wearing them as jewelry, or practicing hands-on healing with laying of stones. Now we move beyond this casual interactions, and enter a sacred sphere of conscious collaboration. You will learn to use Crystals with your Mudras in a specific unifying practice, that will magnify the healing potential with a clear purpose and focus, while elevating you to a higher frequency level.

MUDRAS AND CRYSTALS BECOME YOUR MAGNIFICENT COLLABORATORS IN THE PROCESS OF YOUR SPIRITUAL ASCENSION.

You will discontinue being simply a passive participant and become an active conscious collaborator with your Crystal. It is like you've met a fantastic master of dance. One can watch a skilled dancer and enjoy the perfection of their movement, but it is an entirely different experience if you are invited to dance together, in a pair. Now you "become unified through the power of dance" and transform each other and everyone that has the pleasure of observing you. Your dance translates into a true, synchronized partnership. A similar magic occurs when you consciously work with your chosen Crystals.

To accomplish the multi faceted purpose of this goal, you are required to learn how to consciously communicate on subtle energy realms. This is where the greatest positive and powerful changes ensue. To put is simply, it is where the most fascinating marvels occur… where they can't be seen with a human eyes. By intentionally bringing your focus and individual Soul energy into this practice, the results will be uniquely transformative.

WHEN YOUR SENSES ARE OVERWHELMED, YOUR SURVIVAL MECHANISM THRUSTS YOU INTO A POSITION OF NUMBNESS AND APATHY.

The technique depicted in this book will guide you through this unique, individualized and very specialized experience. You can develop an ability for deep inner communication when merging Mudras and Crystals, but it is essential to understand the most important details. In fact, the Crystal will help you access and connect with your own Higher Consciousness. Your awareness and clarity can reach a much higher level than you imagine, so you can intentionally co-create positive frequencies. This will help you hold on to unwavering peace, regardless of any disturbing and unharmonious frequencies that may appear in your immediate environment, or that you may be unwillingly exposed to.

Is this important, and why do you need this now? It is quite obvious that the world is transitioning through a rather challenging energy shift. This is an ongoing dynamic. Everything that takes place has a profound effect on you.

MUDRAS AND CRYSTALS WILL ENERGETICALLY SHIELD YOUR ENTIRE SUBTLE ENERGY FIELD AND PROTECT YOUR SENSORY ABILITIES.

Because of the current ongoing difficult environmental and world dynamics, our ability to communicate, express, trust, and basically function is gravely affected. We are challenged in overwhelming ways, which can cause sensory numbness with energy depletion. When we are forced to continuously differentiate, recognize and choose what is best for our basic and overall well-being it becomes a constant, unavoidable and tiresome chase. But you must remember, feeling helpless is avoidable. You have the ability to change this dynamic and take charge.

We know that Mudras help you realign, reactivate and cleanse your congested energy currents and sensitive Chakra centers. Crystals magnify these initiated restorative effects and profoundly expand and intensify the self-healing capacity of your entire being. The fusion of Mudras and Crystals will help you unblock the stagnant energy, so that you may redirect it for beneficial and positive purpose. However, it is essential that you consciously participate in this process, and maintain a newly gained state of clarity and peace.

It is always up to each individual to make a decision and move forward while embracing change. In order for the practice of Mudras and Crystals to be optimally effective, you need to be aware of your every thought, desire, energy pattern and weakness. Once you know yourself, Crystals and Mudras become your ideal energy transformation and recharge partner.

**MUDRAS AND CRYSTALS ARE EXTRAORDINARY POWER TOOLS
THAT CAN BE USED PROPERLY
ONLY IF AND WHEN
YOU ARE ABSOLUTELY TUNED - IN
WITH YOUR HEART AND SOUL.**

THE MANY LAYERS OF YOU

Our Energy bodies are incredibly intricate and complex. The seven Chakras and over 72.000 energy currents called Nadis, are interwoven in an energy sphere that contains our many layers and finer sub-layers. Everything and everybody vibrates at a certain frequency level and this affects your energy field, especially if you are weak. When are you most vulnerable?

PHYSICAL VULNERABILITY

You are physically most vulnerable when your frequency is weakened by negative physical states of burn-out, exhaustion, depletion, toxicity, electromagnetic pollution, over-acidity as a result of bad diet, poor physical strength and stamina, and when enduring overwhelming levels of chronic, long-term stress.

MENTAL VULNERABILITY

This is just as open to invasion as your physical condition. When your mental disposition and thoughts are pessimistic and negative in nature, you vibrate at a lower frequency. You are easily swayed and overpowered by a stronger or manipulative frequency. This does not mean higher frequency, but stronger. Such external negative frequency will sway your decisions, influence your thinking and detrimentally affect your confidence. Your mind will fall into a downward spiral of a negative pattern, that will have a counterproductive effect on everything you do or experience.

EMOTIONAL VULNERABILITY

If your emotional body is in a state of grief, unhappiness, while incapable of giving, receiving or practicing self-love, this additional weakened frequency layer will make you more susceptible to outside influences. A lack of emotional strength will cause irrational and self-destructive ill-considered choices in a desperate attempt to fill a void. Every negative disposition and aspect you feel matters and lowers your overall frequency and resilience. Your depleted emotional energy vortex will affect all who come in close contact with you. A positive or negative emotional state has a highly contagious effects on others, especially emotionally fragile people. If your emotional state is weak, it will be easily thrown off balance.

SPIRITUAL VULNERABILITY

The consequences of any of these previously mentioned subtle energy weaknesses make you highly sensitive and unable to resist external negative frequencies. They simply overpower you. This creates an unavoidable pulling-down effect that drains your energy and keeps you on a lower frequency level, that may not be your true natural state. You feel discomfort, unease, lack of support, sense of belonging, security and love. Such a state is a highly undesirable energy drain and promotes spiritual stagnation, loss of focus and lack of desire to pursue your mission. When you lose faith in Divine Universal power and protection, you enter a state of serious spiritual vulnerability. To prevent all these possibilities from occurring, you must understand the importance of your conscious participation and clarity of intention. Only YOU can decide to uplift yourself and change the course. Therefore, before you begin your work with Mudras and Crystals, always take proper time for preparation and tune-in. Remember how intricate, interconnected and complex the invisible ethereal realms and dimensions are. Cherish and protect your delicate self.

Angelite

YOUR INTERACTIONS WITH THE WORLD AND PEOPLE IN IT

All of us have vulnerabilities and carry old wounds. It is imperative that you know and consciously tend to them with a clear desire for recovery and healing. Remember that you benefit from all life experiences, regardless of their positive or negative outcome. Experiences offer a priceless treasure of invaluable wisdom.

If you have a prominent vulnerability or weakness, this will be quite obvious in the subtle energy realms. In such a case, your Aura has an actual opening, a tear, an exposed area, where negative frequencies have open access to your deeper and vulnerable energy core. If your Aura is penetrated, the damaging frequencies will overwhelm your subtle bodies, while reaching further into your core energy matrix. Careless exposure to invasive energies will further upset your inner balance and overall state. And while this sounds quite daunting, it is important for you to be informed so you can help prevent such an occurrence. Avoid all mind altering and addictive substances that weaken and constrict your energy field, making it porous and easily penetrable. These complex energy interactions are triggered and most obvious in personal relationships. It is essential that you surround yourself with healthy and positive frequencies that will expedite the healing of your Aura field.

What can you do? Consciously choose positive physical activities and nutrients to heal your physical body. Select healthy environments and mental activities to strengthen and uplift your mental energy body. Lovingly tend to your emotional needs, release negative patterns to help heal your emotional energy body. Each day dedicate a few minutes to reconnect with your Spiritual anchor. Sometimes we seem to forget how incredibly important are our actions, choices, environment and people we allow near us. Everything has an effect on you, so be wisely selective and acutely aware.

ENERGY FREQUENCY ATTRACTION AND BALANCE

If you have a physical, mental or emotional void, you will be attracted to a person that fills precisely that void, no matter how healthy or dysfunctional they are. Likewise, if you are overly generous, a chronic giver and pleaser, the person attracted to you will have a perfectly matched void, need or desire. A giver usually attracts a taker and vice versa. They will be drawn to your overly extended energy that is felt from miles away. Together, you will resonate as a pair, even if the match is not a healthy one. Once the dynamic inevitably shifts, the delicate balance collapses. A giver becomes less generous in order to conserve their energy, and the overly needy taker feels rejected and ignored. Restoring and establishing a healthy balance will take considerate adjusting. If both partners manage to grow and mend their individual voids, we have a happy end, or shall we say, a good new beginning. If not, your relationship will fall apart and you will embark on a desperate search for the next imperfect match that will fill your void or deficiency. If your ship has a leak, changing passengers won't make any difference. Ideally, each partner has a healthy energy field without majorly depleted or damaged areas, and can attract a healthy equal. If you are energetically balanced, you will attract a balanced partner. Like attracts like.

Rhodonite

MERGING OF AURAS AND INDIVIDUAL FREQUENCIES

We have established that everything and everybody in our environment affects us with their unique frequency. However, someone that you are exceptionally close to, does more than that. They actually intertwine their energy with yours. Your frequencies resonate harmoniously. This way, you can have a loving and positive energy attachment with people that are thousands of miles away, yet the subtle energy connection exists. It is a finer energy frequency of an emotional, mental, or even a deeply spiritual bond.

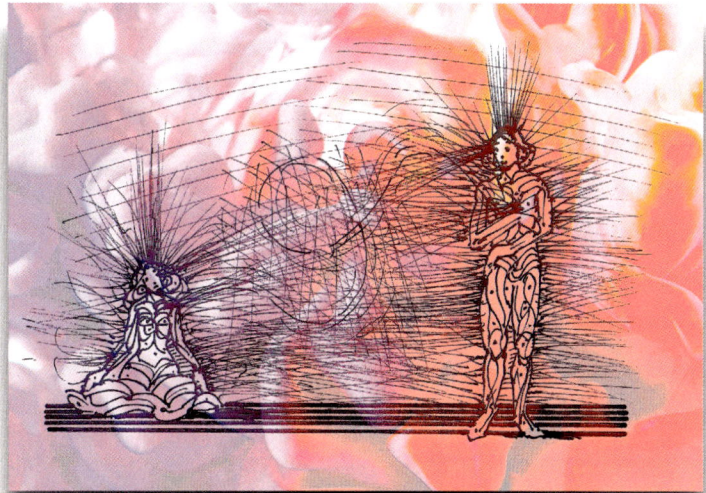

You may be physically apart, but remain energetically connected. You each have your own frequency, but can strongly affect and balance each other, regardless the distance of time and space. If you are in tune with that person, you can intuitively feel their emotions and sense their thoughts, especially when they think of you. These powerful energy attachments between two individuals can be of course also of a more negative or challenging nature. You can help resolve and eliminate conflicting and draining energy connections with the help of Mudras and Crystals. If you are emotionally or intimately very close with someone, your finer energy frequency bodies will merge. This is why it is of utmost importance that you are conscious and carefully selective with whom you merge in such an energetically intimate and binding way. The invisible subtle energy residue of your individual close interactions will remain with you for years. Once such deep and intimate energy link is established, a powerful invisible cord interconnects the two of you for a long lasting bond. This grants the other person access to your energy field in whatever way the nature of your connection was established. Undoing this link requires time, release, letting go of accompanying emotions and if needed, forgiveness.

SUBTLE ENERGY COMPATIBILITY BETWEEN PEOPLE

Most often the two people in a relationship may not have a perfectly matched natural frequency resonance. They have a certain level of compatibility, especially in the beginning of a love relationship, but eventually they will meet a few challenges on the way. If one partner naturally resonates at a higher frequency, they will have to descend a bit, in order to achieve a harmonious resonance together with the partner who naturally resonates at a lower frequency. If the exchange is based on deep love, both partners will interact positively, triggering the highest emotions of love and therefore resonating on a slightly higher frequency than their natural frequency.

Rose Quartz

LOVE ELEVATES US TO OUR HIGHEST ATTAINABLE FREQUENCY POTENTIAL AND BEYOND.

This is especially the case in the beginning of a relationship where strong emotions of love automatically uplift both partner's frequencies. In that moment, they seem perfectly compatible. They are at their highest frequency functioning capacity. But, keep in mind, if one partner is naturally considerably lower in frequency, they will be only capable to sustain this frequency ascension for a limited period of time. Their temporary state of higher frequency is actually their own evolutionary learning process, not the work of the other, higher frequency partner.

This is important to know for all of those who hope to "rescue" or elevate a partner on their own. It is actually the partner alone that has to mature to that point, as this is their individual ascension process. The "rescuer" may have triggered the elevated state with high frequency emotions of love, but this will be difficult to sustain on a permanent basis. Eventually, the weaker partner will most likely descend and return to their natural lower frequency and the pair will become less compatible. It was the new emotion of love that lifted both into a harmonious pairing, but it will eventually shift. This is not necessarily critical, but it is a fact. If the love between them is strong and the lower frequency partner is willing and eager to grow into the higher frequency, the relationship development process may be beautiful and remain sufficiently compatible with occasional disharmonies, which are perfectly common. However, keep in mind, that the partner with a naturally higher frequency will have to descend and suffer the consequences of draining, unharmonious energy states.

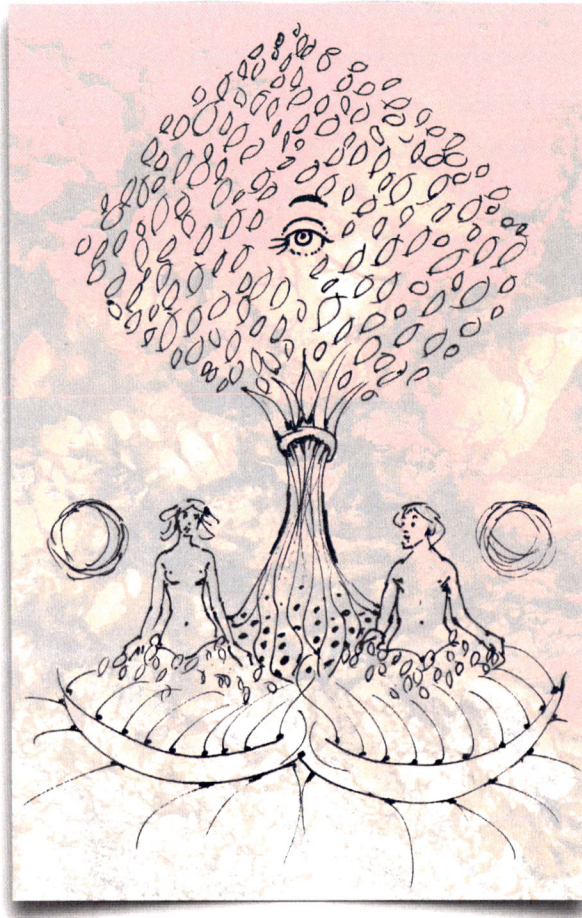

Why? Because one's natural frequency state is earned through lifetimes of the complex ascension process. Descending is not in harmony with the law of the Universe, but ascension is. When you go against your own evolutionary progress, you will experience discomfort, discontent, unhappy, draining and unfulfilled emotional states. This is your Higher Consciousness reminding you, that you need to stay on your path and be true to yourself, your needs, abilities and your life purpose. In the dynamic of intimate or close emotional interaction, your Auras blend and leave an imprint on each other. Hopefully you are compatible, so that the imprint is positive and loving.

UNDERSTANDING THE HEALING PROCESS

In case the interpersonal energy exchange is draining and challenging, the subtle imprint residue will create obstructions, blockages, and congestion in your energy field. These close subtle energy exchanges and bonds may exist between yourself and your lovers, partners, friends, close and far relatives, or people you randomly meet thru your life and towards whom you feel a strong, often inexplicably powerful energetic attraction. Anyone that you have a close energetic connection with, will and can have a subtle energy affect on you.

If the energy exchange is of a positive nature, this is obviously wonderful, uplifting and beneficial to both. If it is challenging, you will have to recognize and properly address this issue. Healing your mutual wounds may occur as a direct result of these close energy interactions. This dynamic may be a predetermined, karmically arranged contract that is a part of your current life's homework. It is something that will need to be resolved and healed in its own time. It is certainly possible that together, you can help heal each other's old wounds. But most often these healing shifts do not happen immediately, and you may carry the challenging energy patterns with you for a certain period of time.

If these faraway past energy imprints are difficult, burdening and disruptive in nature, they will further affect your future choices, behavior, decisions, dispositions and openness to new experiences. This will continue until the patterns are resolved. In fact, every energetic imprint affects your current life in a profound way. You can consciously chose to shift and let go of a negative energy pattern or habit, and establish a new healthy pathway and belief system. It is your purpose to understand, heal and ascend beyond your painful wounds from past relationship experiences, and learn unconditional love. This is an ongoing life-long process, that expands thru all of our countless lifetimes.

I am mentioning these aspects here with a specific purpose, to help you understand and truly decipher your own energy matrix and find a clear vision for your imminent deep inner work. Personal relationships are a fantastic learning opportunity to help us grow. Avoiding these experiences is like avoiding life. In our process and through the technique that you will learn in this book, it is of utmost importance that you become well versed at understanding and sensing the invisible world of frequencies in relation to YOU. Knowing yourself is the key to creating a happy, healthy, fulfilled and content life for yourself. It is also a requirement for deep energy work. You may believe that you know yourself very well, but keep in mind, that you do not know yourself in all possible circumstances or under pressure that may be created entirely from outside influences. You may be a very calm and peaceful person by nature, but an unusual event in your immediate environment may affect you more than you expect or are prepared for.

ALWAYS REMEMBER, THROUGH YOUR LIFE JOURNEY THE FIRST AND MOST IMPORTANT PERSON TO HEAL IS YOU. ONCE THAT IS ACCOMPLISHED, YOU CAN HELP OTHERS IN NEED.

Amethyst

RECOGNIZE THE WOUNDS IN YOUR ENERGY MATRIX

Your vulnerability to environment begins with your own subtle energy constitution. If your subtle energy body is strong, clear of obstructions, and void of energy leaks, you will be able to ward off outside destructive vibrations with great resilience and stamina.

If your energy body is weak and overwhelmed with old or ongoing burdens that drain you off vital life force, you will be incredibly vulnerable to outside influences. Your resistance to negative currents will be weak, and you will become an open target for unwanted energy entities, that will prey on you, eager to live off your vital energy force.

This may sound troublesome, but in order for you to protect yourself in a most profound way, you need to truly understand the complexities of these dynamics. Your old or recent wounds in your energy matrix may expose a literal opening that will easily attract outside influences. If you are not informed of these aspects, you are exposed, defenseless and unaware of the susceptible state you are in.

This occurrence can be completely prevented from ever happening. It can also be healed in the process. What is required is your conscious recognition and awareness of your weaknesses. Before you begin working with Crystals you need to identify your own current state. The level of success in your work with Crystals depends upon this awareness.

CRYSTALS ARE HIGH FREQUENCY MAGNIFIERS AND GENERATORS. MUDRAS ARE POWER TOOLS THAT ACTIVATE YOUR SUBTLE SYSTEM. TO ASSURE A PRODUCTIVE COLLABORATION YOU NEED TO BE PROPERLY PREPARED AND SYNCHRONIZED.

Obviously, Crystals will play a big role in your healing, but this can only begin when you know precisely what aspect of yourself needs to heal. Healing is required on all your levels: physical, emotional, mental and spiritual. All these parts are YOU. This is the principle when you are working with Crystals on your own, and requires you to clearly communicate your needs. This may not be the case if you go to a Crystal healer who will act as the communication guide, intermediary or link. However, our goal is to make you self-sufficient.

In this book, our intention is to enable you to work with Crystals independently, on your own and for your higher good, while consciously participating in the process. Mudras play a very important role in this dynamic, as you will soon learn. Of course the presence of a Crystal in your immediate environment will positively affect you even if you are entirely unaware of your specific needs or subtle energy vulnerabilities. However, your healing will be much more effective, expedited and very precisely targeted when you know where you need help.

KNOW YOURSELF FIRST, AND THEN MY DEAR HEALER, HEAL THYSELF.

Chapter Four
You and Your Crystals

AFFINITY AND COMPATIBILITY

Mudra for Astral Projection with Smoke Quartz

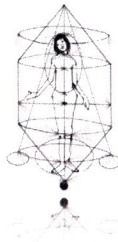

Uniting the Crystal Aura with Your Own

We reviewed these basics human interaction - subtle energy dynamics for one fascinating reason; Crystals work under similar principles when they are in a relationship with you. You and your Crystal are mutually attracted to each other for energetic reasons. But there is one substantial and crucial difference between human relationships and your dynamic with a Crystal:

A Crystal will never deplete you.
It will recharge you and activate your inner Light.

As we learned before, Crystals emit a very high and clear natural frequency, and have in fact their own powerful energy body, an actual Aura field. Their complex energy matrix is perfectly synchronized. When you interact with a Crystal it has higher frequency than you. Thus, you are the one receiving the opportunity and benefit for growth and frequency ascension. Nevertheless, unlike with two people where you can not really "pull" the other person considerably higher in sense of frequencies, this is very different in your interaction with Crystals. When you are open and receptive, a high frequency Crystal can actually elevate your consciousness into a higher frequency state. A Crystal is your stronger positive partner that will uplift you, sustain you and help you heal. In that view, the Crystal can be your rescuer, protector and guide. Your mutual relationship is of great benefit to you and offers immense gifts of helping you access your natural wisdom, inner awareness and states of higher consciousness.

Let's mention another important component about your energetic relationship with the Crystal. This magnificent being resonates at a very clear singular high frequency. We humans do not function like that, that is one of the reasons why our energy frequency is weaker and susceptible to disruptions. Because the Crystal resonates at a higher frequency, your interaction will require a conscious effort on your part in order to be receptive, ascend and resonate in harmony with the Crystal. If you are able to still your mind into a state of receptivity, openness and a desire for ascension, you will allow the frequency of the Crystal to prevail and help you

When you work with Mudras and Crystals,
you are collaborating with a magnificently powerful being
that has the ability to open the gates
into worlds and dimensions unknown to you.

ascend. The Crystal becomes the overpowering and guiding frequency you resonate with.

You are accessing your own field of Higher Consciousness with direct help from the Crystal. Remember, the Crystal offers clarity and a steady high frequency that is unwavering. This is why it is an irreplaceable part in the world of electronics. It is incredibly reliable. When you allow your energy frequency to ascend higher, simultaneously another effect is triggered. Your Aura field blends with the Aura of the Crystal. You work together in harmony and with clarity as one. You enter a state of profound communication. The possibility of this occurrence lies with you.

In a state of optimal calmness, you can receive and understand the knowledge accessible to you. This state is highly sensitive and can not be forced or imagined. It is a very specific state of suspended and exceptional clarity, unwavering access to clear knowledge, free of doubt, need to analyze, or in any way justify the information you receive. It is a state of unequivocal awareness and receptivity beyond the shadow of a doubt. As this may sound simple, it is obviously not for it requires proper preparation, diligent practice, and the purest, most loving and humble of intentions. It demands the ability to open up and surrender in gratitude to a truly divine gift of knowledge and supreme wisdom.

Now, we are one step closer to learning how to achieve the needed and desired state of receptivity and openness, so that you may embark on this magnificent communication journey with your Crystal. This is where Mudras enter into play and contribute with a most important aspect of the technique. Mudras are simply irreplaceable when used in the preparation and advanced interactive process. But first, you need to find your ideal Crystal partner.

DISCERNMENT IN SELECTING A CRYSTAL

Now we are getting into the fascinating experience of interacting with Crystals one on one. Your preparation work, assessment and review of your current state on a deeper energy level will play a decisive role in your success of the future collaboration with Crystals. Create the best circumstances for activating your alert awareness and open your receptivity right from the beginning of your relationship. We addressed the detailed elements of your subtle energy field and interaction dynamics between people. Although your interaction with a Crystal has some fine frequency similarities, there is one prominent and decisive difference. A Crystal will always uplift you and retain its high frequency in a most stable and solid way. A deeper understanding of this synergy requires an activation of your extra sensory abilities, because you will need to communicate with a Crystal in a different, not human "language".

**A CRYSTAL HAS A FREQUENCY AND AN ENERGY FIELD.
A CRYSTAL IS NOT DEAD MATTER,
IT IS A MIGHTY POWERHOUSE AND VERY MUCH ALIVE.**

Extra sensory language can only work when you have utter inner balance and absolute clarity. This principle needs to be followed. Yes, some people can have access to deeper clarity even while they are in a challenging environment, but that requires a well established trained ability in addition to sharp focus. The Mudra practice will help you establish a sense of inner peace and receptivity needed. Be patient with yourself and know that with time this ability will improve.

Now you are ready to find and meet your Crystals. When looking for a Crystal, be cautious and aware of the place where you find it, who handles it and the energy of the environment where it is. Always use your intuition.

FINDING YOUR CRYSTAL

The most important aspect to consider when choosing a Crystal, is how does its energy resonate with you? Your individual frequency will feel attracted to the frequency of a certain Crystal. You can not be attracted to the wrong Crystal, especially if you are aware, open, receptive and consciously looking for a Crystal to work with. Your Crystal will literally send you a beam of light to draw you closer. When you see it, touch it, and feel its energy, this connection will be confirmed. You will feel an immediate attraction and determination to keep it near you. You simply must have it. In fact, it is the essence of that particular Crystal that captivates and resonates with you on a finer subtle energy level. Upon finding the right Crystal, you will sense various uplifting emotions, perhaps amazement at its beautiful appearance, awe at its color nuances, and when holding it in your hands, a sense of connection and affection. You may exclaim "I love it…" and in fact you will fell a sense of loving attraction and infatuation that resembles and reminds you of Love, the highest frequency field. You will not want to let go or be separated from this Crystal and will feel inclined to have it close even if just for decorative purpose, so you may enjoy its beauty.

THE SIZE AND POWER OF YOUR CRYSTAL

When you go thru the process of finding a Crystal, there are a few important things to keep in mind. The healing power of your Crystal is not determined by its size. A smaller Crystal, like the Herkimer Diamond Quartz is quite a powerhouse and vibrates at a very high frequency. In this case a small stone's frequency will be higher than for example that of a Moonstone, even if it is a larger sample. Although a Moonstone has wonderful healing properties on many levels, the actual frequency is lower than that of a tiny Herkimer diamond.

Small but mighty
Herkimer Diamonds

When you are choosing a Crystal, do not get preoccupied with the price. More expensive does not always mean a high quality or high frequency Crystal. Perhaps it is fashionable or in demand at the moment, but it may not be your destined Crystal at all. You may find a phenomenal Crystal for a very fair price. It is most important that the Crystal is compatible with your personal frequency and is what you energetically need at the very precise moment you found each other. Remember to listen to your intuition when selecting your Crystal.

When you include into your Mudra practice a specific Crystal with a desire to achieve a higher state of consciousness, a higher vibration stone would help you accomplish that easier, IF you are receptive. That will of course depend on your individual ability to elevate your consciousness to a higher level. This means that you could have a small Crystal with a high vibration and work wonders within that dynamic. It depends on your ability to receive healing energy and consciously ascend with your Crystal. If you offer a high frequency Crystal to a person with little awareness, they can still benefit, however just to their best receptive capacity.

WHEN SELECTING A CRYSTAL, IT IS NOT ITS SIZE THAT MATTERS, BUT THE INVISIBLE FREQUENCY LEVEL. YOU WILL FEEL A SUBTLE, HARMONIOUS CONNECTION AND AN ENERGY ATTRACTION.

Similarly, you can have a phenomenal computer, but if there's no electricity, it is useless. Or, you can love someone to pieces, but if they are unable to receive your love, there is nothing you can do. A Crystal always offers a steady opportunity for a reliable frequency boost, but it depends how receptive you are. You are working together, in unison. A very large Crystal has a larger Aura that gives it more strength. If you are working with a difficult energy state that requires a lot of clearing, a larger Crystal may be able to endure more, however the Crystal with a higher frequency will elevate you higher. These are the intricate and important details you need to understand, in order to appreciate the complexity of this wondrous technique.

PERFECT CRYSTAL TIMING

A Crystal comes into your life when you need it. At that moment it will offer you what you require and what you are capable of receiving. It is possible that you've had a Crystal for a long while and have not used it yet, and the Crystal simply waited for you to be ready. It could also be a case that you find a Crystal, work with it intensely and then after a while, your mutual assignment is done. You may suddenly feel like gifting a friend with this Crystal which is perfectly fine. Perhaps the Crystal can be of more help to your friend now. Of course some Crystals may stay with you forever. When you give someone a Crystal, they will interact with it in their own best way, and the Crystal will adapt to the needs of the new owner, friend and collaborator. If a Crystal is given to you in friendship or love, it will always carry within the loving frequency of that special intention.

A CRYSTAL IS A MESSENGER OF LIGHT

It is important to understand that a Crystal has a mission and a purpose to spread and magnify the Universal Light. This is where your compatible purpose joins forces and becomes more effectively fulfilled. Likewise it is important to mention that if you find yourself not responding to a Crystal, no matter how appealing in appearance, the Crystal has not chosen you. It did not find compatible energy frequency and the power of that specific Crystal is not accessible to you.

Lemurian Star Seed Quartz

You either choose each other or not, the pairing has to be a mutual, harmoniously compatible organic attraction. Mudras become a fantastic tool to help expand, strengthen and open up your field of receptivity, so that you may recognize and eventually work with your compatible Crystal at the optimal level.

This makes a crucial difference. The key component is your ability to fine tune and recognize the "calling " of the Crystal essence. A Crystal will sense your frequency, attune itself to you and respond to your needs, if it so chooses. So if you find yourself in a Crystal store and someone is encouraging you to purchase a specific Crystal that may be very "valuable", keep in mind that perhaps it will be the smaller, less expensive Crystal without any fancy names, that will be in fact your magical Crystal. See beyond the criteria of this world, and learn to sense its energy with your intuitive heart. Trust your inner guidance. Your Crystal is calling out to you. Listen carefully and you will hear its voice.

PURIFY AND CLEANSE YOUR CRYSTAL

When you have found your favorite and most irresistible new friend – your new Crystal, it is time to establish a new dynamic for your optimal "partnership and collaboration". Before you do anything, it is important to create ideal circumstances for a most promising "launch"of your relationship, so that both of your energies are perfectly aligned, clean and harmonious.

No doubt, your Crystal has been thru a long and fascinating journey before it landed in your hands. Now you need to help clear any residue of its travels and people that touched it, so it can settle into a new environment and find optimal resonance with you. You also need to take into consideration things you don't know, for example who used it before, what was it used for and if it may be drained of vital force, in case it was neglected or shuffled around thru various markets. Consider all these circumstances and focus on providing the perfect environment for the Crystal to get in-tune with the new home and you. The cleansing can be done in a few different ways. You may wash it under cool running water for a few minutes and then place in in the sun. Allow it to receive some sun rays for at least thirty minutes. Afterwards, dry it off gently. Keep in mind, some Crystals should not be immersed or washed in water as they are water soluble. In that case, use any of the other methods. Some Crystals such as Amethyst, should not be placed in direct sunlight, instead use moonlight, or other cleansing methods.

Quartz Cluster

You can submerge a Crystal in sea salt for three hours before use. The sea salt can not be re-used afterwards since it absorbed residual energy. You may also use a Quartz Crystal cluster to cleanse and recharge your new Crystal. Gently place your Crystal on the Quartz Crystal cluster for a while, or permanently. Crystals love natural waters and can also be washed in streams or the ocean, but be careful as they could easily slip out of your hands. Another way to cleanse the Crystal is with a Sage or Cedar Smudge stick. Light the stick and let the cleansing smoke envelop the Crystal for a few minutes. And finally, a very powerful way to recharge a Crystal is to place it under a pyramid structure.

My Crystal Family

HEALING A TRAUMATIZED CRYSTAL

Despite their power, Crystals can get exhausted when neglected, misused, overused, or mishandled. How can this happen? If you use a small Crystal with a weaker frequency for a very considerable energetic assignment or burden, it will not change its frequency level, but it will get depleted. In such a case it will loose its luster and vibrant energy. But a small Crystal with higher frequency will be able to endure more. It is possible to heal Crystals by offering them a good cleansing and opportunity to recharge. Best recharging occurs by placing them on a Quartz cluster or under a pyramid structure. Crystals that are used very often and asked to work repeatedly, need to rest in a place where they are continuously recharged. Sunlight is also a very important element, as is your own care and disposition towards them. Later we shall learn a way to personally recharge them.

DEMATERIALIZATION

It is possible that a Crystal simply vanishes, and not because you misplaced it. Crystals have been know to leave the material plane in order to work in other, higher subtle dimensions.

CAN A CRYSTAL CRACK?

Yes, it often happens that a Crystal can crack after a very challenging healing session, or a piece of Crystal jewelry bursts when it is worn during a particularly overwhelming and challenging energy shift. I have seen it happen! It is quite dramatic and marks the end of that particular Crystal's assignment.

CRYSTAL PLACEMENT

Generally speaking, Crystals love to be placed in the light in your home on the shelves, your bed stand, meditation altar, desk and wherever they can reflect and magnify the light. They will enhance positive energy and bring much light as well as peaceful power to any area where they reside. Don't keep them in the dark, they don't like to be hidden. A darker Crystals should not be placed in direct sunlight for a long time, as their color will fade.

MAINTAINING YOUR CRYSTAL

Your Crystal is an amazing being and requires your attention. In order to help your Crystals thrive and maintain their optimal frequency so you two can accomplish various assignments, you need to offer them cleansing water, sunlight, kind attention and much love.

Ammolite

UNDERSTANDING THE SUBTLE QUALITIES OF YOUR CRYSTAL

As we mentioned before, when the timing is right, your Crystal and you will find each other. Once you do, you will want to communicate as much as possible. Keep in mind that it may not be immediately revealed to you what mission your Crystals has with you. When you are ready, the assignment will become clear at a particular predestined moment.

I encourage you to follow your intuition when searching for a Crystal and focus less one the specific purpose you want the Crystal for. You may not know the best pathway to overcome an issue, or the true source of your challenge. Another factor is that the place where you purchase the Crystal may not offer the information that will match your needs or expectations.

Let's say you feel attracted to a very specific Crystal while you wish to receive some help in your relationships. This Crystal may not be considered ideal for that purpose, if its general description is that of a Rainbow Crystal. However, perhaps this Crystal will teach you about the relationship issues that you are facing and therefore this is precisely the Crystal you need. Trust your intuition more than the description or name of the Crystal. Your subconscious knows better what you truly need and where your energy essence is weak or requires healing frequency. Your conscious mind is not aware of subtler issues. What matters is your individual synchronicity with a specific Crystal. It has to come from an organic intuitive place and not from a mental association with a "category" of a Crystal.

There are specific Crystals that will offer an easier insight into past lives or your future. However, if you don't resonate with this Crystal the results won't be fruitful. A rare Crystal that is supposed to hold ancient wisdom may not offer you any information at all. Why?

A CRYSTAL THAT HOLDS RARE KNOWLEDGE IS PROTECTED. TO GAIN ACCESS TO ITS TREASURE, REQUIRES AN ENERGY KEY THAT IS HIDDEN IN A CHOSEN PERSON.

May I suggest that you learn to enjoy the unique Crystals you already have in your personal home collection regardless of their specific category. I am quite sure you have a few Crystals that you've owned for a while. Concentrate and learn to work with them without expectation, but with energy synchrony, mutual respect and love.

Begin this journey simply with an open heart and take baby steps of understanding and recognizing Crystals that may be ideal for you. It would defeat the purpose if you embark on a hunt for a rare Crystal, only to learn that you can't even begin to understand the complexity of information or receive any specific answers you are seeking. Your perfect Crystal is most likely already in your home and your life.

Understand your limitations while respecting the Crystal kingdom. Allow the Crystal to "call you" so that you can embark on this adventure together with whatever Crystal is ideal for you at this particular time. Simplicity may be the key. Remember, the simplest looking Crystal can hold mighty power and wisdom that is incredibly important for you at this very particular time in your life. It is ready to help you beyond your imagination. Here are some examples of beautiful Crystals that are wonderful to use in your Mudra Crystal practice. The Bridge Quartz below is a Barnacle, meaning it is a larger Crystal with smaller Crystals attached to it. A Barnacle Crystal is an old soul, nurturing younger incoming souls.

Bridge & Barnacle Quartz

Ruby

Pietersite

Golden Healer Tangerine Quartz

Charoite

HOW TO HOLD THE CRYSTALS
DURING YOUR MUDRA PRACTICE

Each Mudra position needs to be practiced correctly and every small detail matters. When using Crystals, keep the same formation of the Mudra as you would in regular practice and adjust the posture as depicted in each practice instruction. Relate to your Crystal as an equal and active participant, be conscious of its powerful energy and stabilizing effects. A Crystal works with you in most intricate and complex ways. In order to register this vibrational merging properly, be very attention and patient in adjusting the Mudra position properly and precisely.

A FEW BASIC MUDRA AND CRYSTAL HAND POSTURES

MUDRA PRACTICE AND CRYSTAL SHAPES

The Mineral kingdom has an incredible family of countless magnificent specimens. Crystals and minerals are fascinating, captivating, and some quite extraordinarily beautiful. All are appointed with truly powerful transformative energies. Some Crystals vibrate at higher frequencies than others, but all carry unique qualities and energies and it would be quite impossible to describe them all in this book. We are concentrating on Mudras and Crystals as a multi faceted healing modality and how you can best take advantage of this marvelous pairing.

I encourage you to pay attention and observe if a specific Crystal appeals to you more than the other, whether it is for reasons of color, shape or simply a personal affinity. These particular preferences are not to be dismissed. In due time you will most likely discover why a certain Crystal appeals to you. It is calling you with a sweet silent whisper, as you carefully search for your new treasured friend. Allow yourself to explore and intuitively recognize which group of Crystals may ideally suit your needs. This will most likely change over time.

Crystals come in countless shapes and unusual formations. For our purpose of a most effective Mudra and Crystal practice, here are a few most typical shapes that you can find.

Rose Quartz Sphere

CRYSTAL SPHERE

Crystal spheres are a wonderful addition to Mudra practice and have a wide, harmoniously dissipated energy reach. You can easily use smaller size spheres for intricate Mudra positions and a bit large sizes for Mudras that require more movement. Their weight is going to add an extra sense of generating energy and will help magnify your overall energy field.

POINT

The many versions of Crystal points can be used in endless ways with Mudras that require an extended finger placement to help amplify the focal point of energy. Direct the Crystal point in the direction where you wish to create the additional flow of energy. You can also use a Crystal point in Mudra positions when wrapping your hand around the Crystal into a fist, or when placing it between spread out fingers.

WAND

Crystal wands have a similar effect as Crystal points, in addition to being a great scanning tool. They direct the healing energy in a straight target line with the tip of the wand helping you aim the healing energy. You can use them with Mudras in different ways, depending on their size, but a palm size wand is ideal for a Mudra practice that requires various spread out finger positions.

PYRAMID

Crystal pyramids are sacred geometry formations that are great generators of high frequency energy. They can be used in Mudra practice positions with clenched palms to help you absorb the energy and recharge at a faster pace. When used with Mudras in wide open hand positions, the pyramid helps generate a large energy field around your energy body that enforces the natural etheric shield.

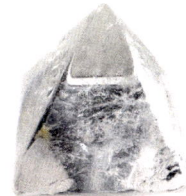

PALM AND PILLOW STONE

Crystal palm and pillow stones offer another ideal shape for your Mudra practice. They fit comfortably into the palm of your hand and allow you to hold Mudras in perfect positions while including the many benefits of Crystal healing and regenerating presence.

HEART

Crystal hearts are ideal for use with Mudras that promote harmony, love, inner security, confidence and self-care. When healing your heart, use this Crystals to reintroduce the healthy principles of an equally balanced exchange of giving and receiving love, cultivating compassion, self-love and inner peace.

CLUSTER

Crystal clusters come in countless shapes and unusual formations. For the purpose of Mudra practice, clusters need to be small in size so you can hold them comfortably and soak up all the healing energy they offer. They are excellent for eliminating negative energy states and can be used in combinations with Mudras specific for that purpose. They are also ideal for recharging your crystal collection and help keep it cleansed and recalibrated. Just place the smaller crystals on the cluster and allow them to replenish.

EGG

Crystals eggs are wonderful for combining with Mudras that evoke your natural sense of creativity, help bring ideas into fruition and create a space conducive to realizing your desires. They are especially potent with Mudras that promote abundance and prosperity. Crystal eggs are easy and comfortable to hold in any Mudra position with clasped hands.

SHIVA LINGHAM

These Crystals are very specific for use with Mudras that address the challenges of the lower three Chakras. The shape is similar to regular egg, however it is a bit more elongated. A smaller size version will easily fit into the palm of your hand.

WORRY THUMB STONE

Crystal worry stones or thumb stones have a special large thumb-sized indentation where you can place your thumb for an extra sense of comfort and perfect merging with your Crystal. They can be used with Mudras where your thumb is required to connect with another fingertip.

MASSAGE WAND

Crystal wands that are used as massage tools are usually curved which makes them perfectly suited for Mudra practice that requires hand on hand placement, palm covering the entire stone and resting on lower arm, or palm of other hand. They are very powerful in energy direction and can be used with Mudras that address issues of comfort, reflection, higher states of consciousness and deeper insight.

CUBE

Crystal cubes come in many variations. For Mudra practice, select cubes that have soft edges and are small in size, fitting nicely into the very center of your palm. They can be very grounding and are ideal for use with Mudras that promote stability, abundance, and prosperity.

TUMBLED STONES

Crystal tumbled stones are wonderful to use in many Mudra combinations. They are ideal to help you learn discernment while exploring the effect of various stones and use them with Mudras that help you raise awareness, intuition, inner guidance and easy access to higher states of consciousness. Each one of us has unique needs and Crystal tumble stones will help you find your ideal Crystal collaborators.

PENDULUM

A Crystal pendulum can be used with Mudras for guidance and wisdom. You can hear your inner answers when your mind is calm and still. Hold the pendulum in your hands during the Mudra practice and work with it afterwards to help confirm a personal question. First use it with a Mudra, so you can synchronize your own and Crystal's energy fields in order to access information you desire much faster and easier.

MALA

Crystal malas are prayer beads used for counting mantras. You can use them with Mudra for Divine worship, inner guidance, higher states of consciousness and for evoking energy protection. Practice Mudra in stillness while holding the mala in your hands. Afterwards, count the beads as you sing, speak or whisper the mantra listed with the Mudra of your choice. You will magnify and activate the powerful resonance field created between the mala Crystals and yourself.

CABOCHON

Crystal cabochon stones are polished and shaped with one curved and one flat side. These Crystals are often used for laying of the stones on body in Crystal therapy sessions, or for decorative and jewelry purposes. You can use them with Mudras in countless possible ways, as long as they fit snugly into the palm of your hand and have no pointy edges that interfere with your Mudra practice.

SELECTING THE CRYSTAL SHAPE

Mudras can be practiced with any shape of Crystal. What matters is your understanding of the specific Crystal, the unique qualities is holds, and how it can best assist you. Select Mudras that are specifically aligned with the qualities of your Crystal. This will create a magnified energy field that will speed up and enhance your desired effects. For example; when using Smoky Citrine Quartz, you could combine Mudras that assist your depleted mental states, help improve self-esteem and confidence, diminish fear, heal your nervous system or cellular disorders, access your inner vision and protect you from electromagnetic pollution. By using the specific abilities of your Crystal with corresponding Mudras, you will enjoy the powerful benefit of two ideally matched subtle energy collaborators.

Sapphire

Chapter Five

Encoding Your Crystals

INITIATION

Mudra for Balanced Speech with Quartz Crystal Double Pointed Wands

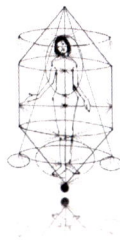

YOUR PREPARATION AND PRACTICE SPACE

In the beginning of your practice, the right environment is of crucial importance. In order to connect with the Crystal energy properly, you will always require a peaceful area without distractions. Create an ideal space for this interaction. Even if you are an experienced Mudra or meditation practitioner, find surroundings that are free of disturbances. Developing a truly deep understanding of the delicate energy interaction between a Crystal and yourself will require time, patience and dedication. Approach this process with clarity of mind and an open heart. Countless benefits shall follow.

Establish a regular location for your practice, where no one will disturb you. Make sure to wait an hour after a big meal, and have no pending pressing matters that await. Your mind needs to have an opportunity to truly let go. Sit comfortably with a straight spine, shoulders down, long neck and begin to concentrate on your breath. Always breathe through the nose, inhaling and exhaling at a slow pace. Place both of your hands on your stomach-solar plexus area, and begin. With each inhalation expand this area and with each exhalation, gently contract it. Continue for a few minutes while relaxing deeper with each breath. Proper breathing will heal you, help you release pain, discomfort, ease tension, and any negative energy congestion that may be stuck in your subtle energy body. The more you oxygenate your system, the better.

WORKING WITH MUDRAS AND CRYSTALS IS A PRIVILEGE. THEY WILL OPEN YOUR NATURAL PERCEPTION AND HELP YOU MAINTAIN A HIGHER STATE OF AWARENESS ESPECIALLY IN TIMES WHEN YOU NEED TO CONQUER A CHALLENGE.

OPEN YOUR MIND AND HEART

Every time you want to establish a new healthy habit, you carry a certain expectation, a goal or intention. This inspiring and hopeful thinking pattern helps you install a new discipline. Set a clear goal, such as implementing a healthy eating habit so you will feel happy and comfortable in your body. That image is your objective and keeps you going thru the challenging beginning when the process requires true strength and determination. Another example would be preparing for a difficult confrontation, or launching a creative endeavor. In each of those cases you have a clear vision of your desired outcome. If you yearn for a loving relationship, this is your goal and the process begins with you acknowledging and consciously opening your energy field so you can connect with the right partner. In all of these cases you are consciously opening your mind and your heart, so that you are receptive and welcoming to all the blessings Universe will send your way.

WHEN YOU KNOW WHAT YOU WANT OR NEED, ASK FOR IT, AND YOU SHALL RECEIVE. BE OPEN, RECEPTIVE AND ALLOW THE UNIVERSE TO SURPRISE YOU.

Your conscious participation

The first level of conscious presence we need to master is within your physical self. You are aware of your physical body, energy level and your needs and desires. This is what you are connected with in a very tangible and obvious way. Your physical body is your outer layer, the coarsest energy field of your being. Your physical condition is a direct result of your natural genetics, environmental factors as well as your subtle energy body's ability for a healthy flow and release of toxic congestion. All your energy layers are interconnected, for you cannot separate your physical body from your mind, or your emotions. Concentrate on all levels of your being, still your body, mind and emotions and systematically distance yourself from the outer world. Enter a meditative state and explore inner realms, invisible to the human eye.

Understand and know that every healing process requires your absolute participation. This is an intricate a part of your soul's evolutionary journey. When you are addressing a subtle energy imbalance, which is often the root cause of a physical illness, your positive emotional and mental disposition become of crucial importance. Your conscious engagement is also decisive whenever you are undergoing a traditional healing treatment. If your disposition is positive, the treatment has a better chance of being successful. If you are an energy healer, you know the importance of your client's mindful participation.

Clarity of Intention in the healing process

I remind you that the practice of Mudras and Crystals is a complimentary healing modality and is not in any way a replacement for medical treatment. It is harmonious with whatever treatment you are currently following or undergoing, be it traditional, alternative or complementary. You can use Mudras and Crystals as a holistic healing partner. It will help you maintain an overall high frequency state to help facilitate and promote any healing process. It is helpful to be in attunement with the highly sophisticated nature of the Crystal, so you may understand its messages and recognize various energy nuances or shifts. Strive to be a conscious participant in all areas of your life, special concerning your wellbeing. When working with Crystals, you can't expect to sit down, blindly ask a question and immediately receive a profound answer. You need to be properly attuned and receptive before "collaborating" with a Crystal. Eliminate any negative inner dialogue. A simple affirmation such as: "I can do that!" will open your Aura field. You will attract and accomplish what you have announced is your reality. This is the power of self-identification. When working with Crystals, be clear of your intention so that they can effectively help you.

Only you have access to your mind's reprograming codes and can consciously choose to change them. Only you know what emotional attachments you carry and can consciously choose to release them. Only you truly sense what is physically uncomfortable for your body and can consciously eliminate it. By taking full responsibility for your well being, you are activating conscious healing.

CRYSTAL PROGRAMMING CODES

Keep your established practice space energetically clean, protected and disturbance free. Clear away any negative energies that may be left over from challenging people or past events. Use a sage smudge stick, open windows to allow fresh air circulation, and remove any items that are energetically bothersome. This will help facilitate an energetically receptive space for your spiritual work. When you feel centered, balanced and peaceful, you may begin the process of encoding your Crystal. If you are programming your Crystal for the very first time, you need to define your clear intention with integrity and mutual respect.

YOUR PURE INTENTIONS AND PLEDGE TO THE LIGHT

Whenever you are opening your energy field to receive energy or information, you need to assure your work with Crystal remains protected in the Light. I recommend that you make a firm and clear request for the brightest, purest and highest Divine Light to envelop, protect and guide you. Always work with true and loving intentions

**THE CRYSTAL IS A MAGNIFICENT MASTER OF LIGHT.
IN ORDER TO WORK WITH IT, MASTER YOUR OWN INNER LIGHT.**

Your intentions must be very pure. A person with negative notions will not receive the desired response because negative thought patterns are not compatible with the unequivocally stable high frequency of the Crystals. They are the natural empowering facilitators and guardians of ancient knowledge and wisdom. You can communicate with them only by elevating your frequency to your highest level.

Proceed thru the beginning steps of your collaboration. In your mind or out loud repeat the following clear affirmations and declarations of your intent. Be conscious of your communication and clear with your pledge.

INITIATION AND DEDICATION

**"I CALL UPON THE HIGHEST POWERS
AND OPEN MY HEART TO THE UNIVERSAL LIGHT FORCE.**

**I CALL UPON MY SPIRIT GUIDES
FOR THEIR PROTECTION, GUIDANCE AND LOVE.**

**LET THIS CRYSTAL HEAL, GUIDE AND SHIELD ME,
WHILE REVEALING THE ANSWERS I SEEK.**

**I AM ETERNALLY PROTECTED BY THE INFINITE LIGHT
AND UNCONDITIONAL LOVE OF THE UNIVERSE."**

MUDRA OF DIVINE WORSHIP

Now you are ready to proceed with your Crystal Programming Codes Initiation process. Place the Crystal between your palms in the Mudra of Divine Worship. Feel your merged energy expand and magnify. Consciously connect with the Divine Universal force. Take your time, for this process is most sensitive and the effectiveness depends on your ability to be absolutely clear with your intention. Call on the Universal Light and imagine an invisible bubble of lightness and bliss allowing your mind to travel beyond earthly limitations.

Sit with a straight back, shoulders down. Lift up your hands and place your palms together. Hold them in front of your heart, elbows comfortably away from body. Feel the energy in your palms and your inner awareness expand while consciously connecting with Crystal energy. Sit still, breathe long, deep and slow and concentrate on your Third Eye for at least three minutes.

BREATH: LONG, DEEP AND SLOW THRU NOSE.

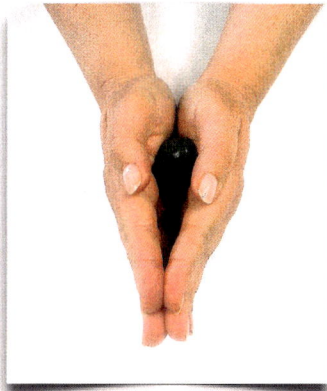

ANY AND ALL INFORMATION GAINED THROUGH THE CRYSTAL IS TO BE USED ONLY WITH THE BEST AND PUREST OF INTENTIONS AND ALWAYS IN HUMBLE AND RESPECTFUL ACCORDANCE WITH THE DIVINE LAW.

This high frequency healing modality is most effective when applied with conscious respect and higher understanding. All your intentions begin with an awareness of your inner truth. A Crystal is a living being and will not respond to you or allow you to access its power, unless it chooses to do so. Respect this highly evolved living essence. You will enjoy lasting gifts and blessings from these otherworldly beings when you treat them with utmost reverence, hear their subtle energy message and honor their powerful will. The Crystal longs to find its proper human match, so it may fulfill its mission. Always strive to work in devotion and harmony with the Universe and all its beings.

AWAKENING THE CRYSTAL

Since the Crystal is a higher frequency being, it certainly responds to sound frequency. Sometimes gentle sounds can be used as a Crystal awakener. The Crystal is not asleep, but it will function in a very different way if it is sitting forgotten on a shelf, or if you work with it in a loving manner. When you begin working with a Crystal you have never used before, it presents an ideal occasion to stimulate it with and awakening sound as a clear signal that you recognize its presence and are inviting it to collaborate. Your Crystal will respond to the sound of Tibetan or crystal bowls, gentle bells, gongs and very fine strings. You can play any of these instruments in a soft and delicate way near the Crystal to evoke a strong harmonious resonance. The Crystal will retain the healing frequency of the sound, which will remain impressed within its structure. This may be perceived by you in a subtle way later, when you meditate with the Crystal.

CHARGING THE CRYSTAL

As I mentioned before, the best way to charge a Crystal is with sunlight, moonlight, or by placing it on a Crystal cluster. You can also lovingly surround the Crystal in golden and white light, while consciously visualizing a beam of Light from your Third Eye center.

PROGRAMING FOUNDATION SET-UP

Before you get very specific about your desired outcome with your Crystal, create a strong, unwavering and protected foundation. This entails you clearly stating the following:

"MAY DIVINE LIGHT PROTECT ME AND THIS CRYSTAL MAY WE BE ABLE TO WORK IN PERFECT ATTUNEMENT WITH THE DIVINE WILL AND FOR THE GOOD OF ALL."

MUDRA FOR OPENING THE THIRD EYE

You may now use this wondrous Mudra
for Crystal program imprinting of your desired intention.

Close your eyes, bring the Crystal to your Third Eye or Crown center and feel complete connection with the image, affirmation and the reality you wish to establish. Direct this clear energy into the Crystal and remain focused for a few minutes. Clearly and perfectly visualize your needs fulfilled. Transfer this desired program into the Crystal. After a few moments you will intuitively feel the transmission is complete.

You may now place the Crystal onto a specially designated spot. Be patient and allow the Universal energies to act in accordance with the Divine law. When you are working in close energy dynamic with a Crystal, you are establishing a Soul connection. In order for it to remain pure, it is essential that you understand the principle of attraction and affirmation. The Universe will always fulfill your needs, so be clear to differentiate between desires which reflect your attachments, or your basic needs for a happy, healthy and abundant life.

**DESIRES BASED IN EGO WILL ALWAYS
TEACH US A PAINFUL LESSON.
HOWEVER, YOUR HEARTFELT DESIRES
IN HARMONY WITH YOUR SPIRIT'S ASCENSION
WILL BE SUPPORTED, ACCEPTED
AND GRANTED IN DUE TIME.
HAVE FAITH.**

CLARITY OF YOUR PROGRAMING

For an optimal collaboration with your Crystal, you need to have utmost clarity when conveying your precise instructions. If you are unclear or hesitant in your communication, you can not expect the desired results. Formulate an exact affirmation that precisely describes the nature of your desired programming. Here are a few examples:

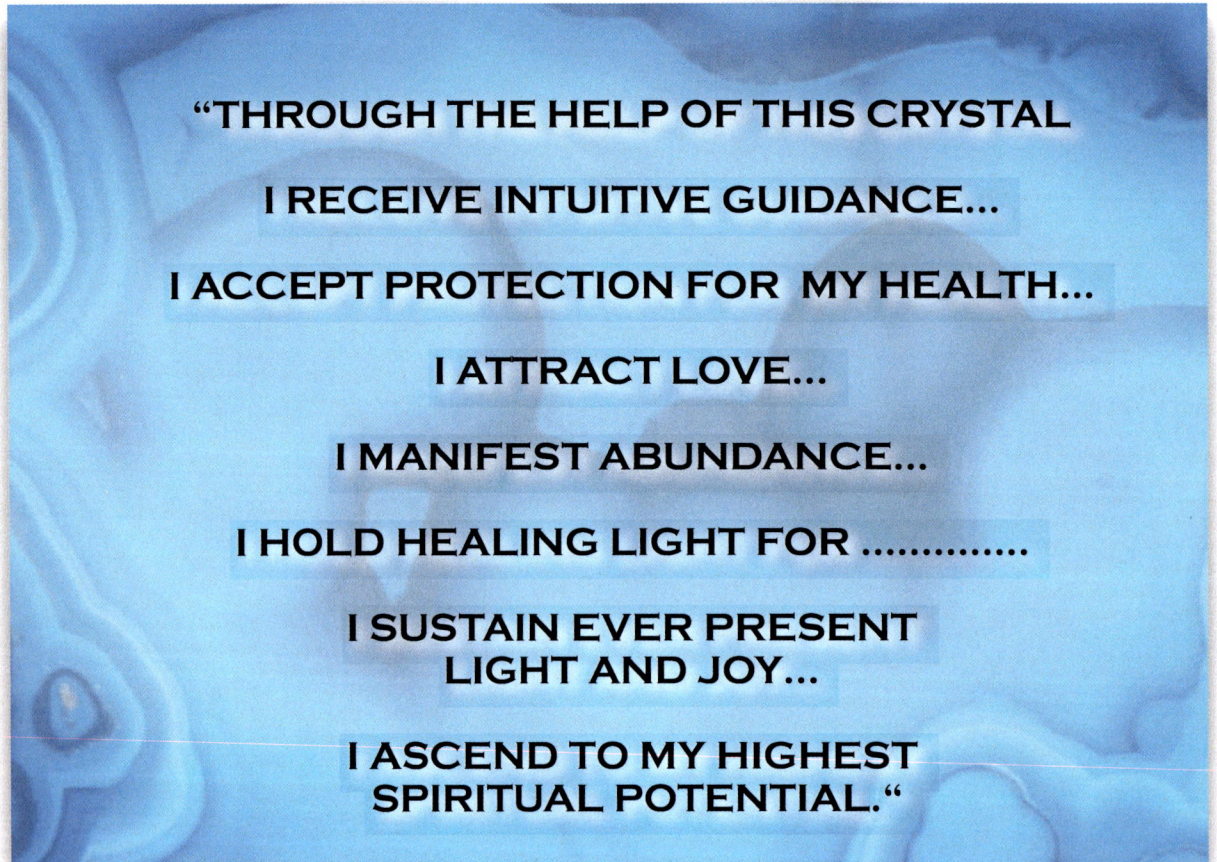

> "THROUGH THE HELP OF THIS CRYSTAL
>
> I RECEIVE INTUITIVE GUIDANCE...
>
> I ACCEPT PROTECTION FOR MY HEALTH...
>
> I ATTRACT LOVE...
>
> I MANIFEST ABUNDANCE...
>
> I HOLD HEALING LIGHT FOR ....
>
> I SUSTAIN EVER PRESENT LIGHT AND JOY...
>
> I ASCEND TO MY HIGHEST SPIRITUAL POTENTIAL."

Repeat this affirmation out-loud or in a whisper. It is most important that you say it with utter conviction, without a shred of hesitation or doubt. Affirm it with complete confidence and trust that the Universe hears you and the Crystal recognizes and understands your clear request to fulfill your needs. Hold the Crystal between your palms in Mudra of Divine Worship, take your time, while slowly and with conviction repeat the affirmation at least twenty times. Visualize the outcome and positive effects of the program you are implementing.

Chapter Six

Mudras & Crystals

CHAKRA SEQUENCE SET

Mudra for Universal Energy & Chakra Scale Crystals

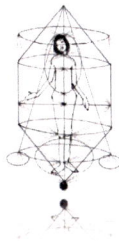

ADVANCED CHAKRA HEALING APPROACH

Nowadays Chakra work has gained in overall popularity, however I feel that much of it is misleading and counterproductive. In my experiences over the past few decades, I have meet countless enthusiastic clients, holistic practitioners, and students that understand the basic principles of the Chakra system. However, they often declare how they plan to "work on a specific Chakra". While this may sound like a good idea, it does not necessarily promise optimal benefits. Why? The truth is that Chakra work is not as simplistic as it may seem and this approach dramatically strays away from any kind of holistic overview.

You are not really defining your challenge by proclaiming "My Third Chakra is out of alignment." Third Chakra is the home of so many variable emotional states, that working in such a general way won't necessarily prove effective and helpful at all. You need to have clear answers to your current needs. This concept applies to all deep and effective Chakra work. Yes, your energy states and associated emotional dispositions can be evaluated in Chakra order, however, I suggest you stay with a clear problem-solution approach. To put it simply, you need to get considerably more specific than just attributing all your issues to one Chakra. This will not help you recognize and resolve your core challenge. Instead, simply ask yourself what is your current and most challenging emotion and then proceed to explore which Chakras are affected. Remember this fact: when one or more Chakras are out of balance, all of your other Chakras are affected as well. You can not expect to have everything working perfectly while having only one isolated area out of alignment. You are one body and your Chakra system is interconnected.

> **OUR CHAKRAS WORK AS ONE UNIFIED ENERGY BODY FOR THAT REASON WE NEED TO TEND TO ALL OF THEM EQUALLY. ANY LOCALIZED CHAKRA DISHARMONY REVERBERATES THROUGH ALL OTHER CHAKRAS. AIM TO BALANCE YOUR ENTIRE CHAKRA SYSTEM.**

The Chakra system is an important and helpful orientation guide to help you find a clear answer when searching for the source of a challenging energy, emotional or mental state. Deepening your knowledge of the various Chakras and how they interrelate and affect your life will reveal answers to countless self-exploratory questions. For that purpose, it is very important to learn the very basics of what each Chakra represents so we can gradually expand this knowledge into finer, subtler areas, where the deep and truly complex answers hide. This way, you will begin to see incredible logic and an order to your subtle energy body work. Your efforts will be repaid with timely and most positive results.

If we search for the essential emotion that is the main culprit of countless challenging issues, the answer is fear. There are numerous emotions that are based on, associated with, or a direct consequence of fear. This requires deeper self-examination. Fear penetrates up and down our Chakra scale and quickly affects every area of our being. Fear is a state that instantly lowers our frequency level and increases our vulnerability to negative energy. When fear holds a stronghold in its home - the Third chakra, we are fearful of fear itself. If that inner state is not recognized and paid attention to, it will move and expand everywhere it possibly can.

MANIFESTATION OF FEAR IN YOUR SEVEN MAIN CHAKRAS:
I. FEAR FOR SURVIVAL
II. FEAR OF REJECTION
III. FEAR OF LOSING CONTROL
IV. FEAR OF A HEARTBREAK
V. FEAR OF SPEAKING THE TRUTH
VI. FEAR OF THE UNKNOWN
VII. FEAR OF GOD'S ABANDONMENT

CLARITY OF CHAKRA DIVISION AND FUSION

Deep seated fear may originate from parental imprint in childhood, or a past life Soul memory. Therefore pointing out which Chakra is the source of a problem, is not as simple as it may seem. It is a complex issue that requires careful consideration.

Looking at the opposite side of the spectrum, the absolute contrast to fear is Love. Lack of love will cause depletion in any or all Chakra centers. A person without love will live in various states that are closer related to emotions of fear. This manifestation will depend on their life situation, such as fear of loosing power, fear of abandonment, fear of rejection, fear of being seen for who they are, fear of obscurity, fear of irrelevance, fear of illness, or fear of death…all these fears have a clear indication of lack of love. If you examine your fear, you will often find its origins related to survival, abandonment and the ultimate source of all fears - fear of death. In a positive and healthy energy state you are functioning in the frequency of Love. An abundance of love will help all Chakras thrive no matter how one is situated in the world from the material or safety perspective. A person with bare necessities living humbly, may glow with love, exhibit excellent health, confidence and a great disposition towards life in general.

Chakra division into lower and upper region will help you discern the distinction between two main opposites: living in fear and functioning at the frequencies of the lower three Chakras, or living in loving devotion and functioning at the frequency of the upper four Chakras, recognizing the higher purpose of your life. Crystals are high frequency beings that are working in higher realms. They are Light, hope, timelessness, and Love. Working with them will facilitate your ascension process to their frequency level. You can use the Crystals to harmonize all your Chakras, while focusing on your ascension process. When consciously shining your inner Light through all your actions, you are sharing it with all that come near you, as is your true purpose.

WHEN YOU MOVE INTO THE FREQUENCY OF THE UPPER CHAKRAS YOU GAIN THE ABILITY TO LOVE UNCONDITIONALLY.
YOUR SOUL IS ASCENDING, SO IT MAY EVENTUALLY RETURN HOME.

Once you have completed the programming initiation of your Crystal, you have established a mutually enforced energy connection field that envelops your entire being. We have reviewed the basic dynamics of Chakra ascension process, and you are now ready for intricate, intentional and exciting deep energy work.

First Chakra

REPRESENTS: Survival, food, shelter, courage, will, vitality, foundation, thriving
LOCATION: Base of spine **COLOR:** Red **AROMA:** Frankincense **KEY AGE:** 1
DESIRES: Security, stability, wealth, territory, strength, stamina, endurance, possessions
CHALLENGES: Endangered survival, greed, delusion, excess, fear of death, violence

CRYSTALS: Andalusite, Andradite Garnet, Aragonite, Black Actinolite, Black Opal, Black Sapphire, Brown Zircon, Carnelian, Cuprite, Fire Agate, Garnet, Hawk's Eye, HematiteRed & Brown & Black Jasper, Red & Brown Jade, Red Agate, Red Aventurine, Red Beryl, Red Bloodstone, Red Calcite, Red Phantom Quartz, Red Sardonyx, Red Serpentine, Red-black Obsidian, Ruby Aura Quartz, Smoky Herkimer, Smoky Quartz, Stichtite, Sunstone, Tourmaline

This Chakra is your foundation, base and the ground you stand on. The stability of your parental family unit leaves an energy imprint on this Chakra in the first year of your life. First Chakra reveals your existential confidence in succeeding on your life path. Regenerating this center requires your examination of what feels weak and how you can mend, strengthen, and consciously activate your naturally given ability for survival. This may be easier said than done, especially regarding financial matters. But if you make an effort and have an intention to work for the good of all, the Universe will always provide for you. It may be a bit different from what you envisioned or expected, but you will be guided, doors will open and resources will come. The question is, will you be able to recognize and accept the Universe's help? This will depend on the receptivity of your first Chakra. Recharge it in nature, relax near a body of water and release your worry. Reflect on your heart's wishes, for in order to move and ascend towards your heart, you have to learn how to listen to it.

> **THE EARTH IS YOUR HOME, IT PROVIDES EVERYTHING YOU NEED.**
> **GROUND YOURSELF, SO YOU CAN PURSUE YOUR LIFE PURPOSE.**
> **THE UNIVERSE WILL SUPPORT YOU AND OPEN ALL DOORS.**

Using Crystals with intention to strengthen this Chakra is very effective, because they are steady, reliable, resilient and vibrant with grounding life force. Feel their presence and unconditional love. Be still, tune in, and make a conscious effort to connect with their Soul energy. Remember, the size of the Crystal does not matter, it is the essence, frequency and character that are decisive. Existential security is the essential need of your first Chakra. In order to attract and manifest abundance, you have to believe it is possible. Proclaim your Divine right to abundance and fulfillment of your needs. You came into this world a helpless child and the Universe provided you with parents. However they functioned, this was your path. Likewise, today and every day, you are provided for. Know this without a doubt in your mind and heart. With the help of this Mudra you can activate your ability to manifest abundance.

MUDRA FOR ATTRACTING ABUNDANCE

Sit with a straight back, keep your shoulders down, nice and relaxed. Place a medium or a few smaller Crystals in the palm of each hand. Lift the hands up, elbows bent, palms are at shoulder level, turned up towards the sky. Inhale and open the palms stretching all fingers while holding the Crystals. Hold for a few moments. Exhale and close your hands while clasping the Crystals, again hold for a few moments. Visualize the Universal force magnified by the Crystal flowing into your hands, while absorbing the energy of abundance. Practice for three minutes.

BREATH
LONG, DEEP AND SLOW THRU YOUR NOSE

MANTRA
SAT NAM *(Truth Is God's Name, One in Spirit)*

AFFIRMATION
I THRIVE, I DESERVE, I BELONG, I PROSPER

Second Chakra

REPRESENTS: Creativity, sex, procreation, family, inspiration
LOCATION: Sexual organs **COLOR:** Orange **AROMA:** Jasmine **KEY AGE:** 2
DESIRES: Sensory stimuli, pleasure, creative expression, sexual relations, attention, approval
CHALLENGES: Addiction, restlessness, confusion, anxiety, over activity, jealousy, envy

CRYSTALS: Blue Tiger's Eye, Carnelian, Fire Opal, Menalite, Orange Jade, Orange Phantom Quartz, Orange Selenite, Orange Spinel, Orange Zicron, Red Garnet, Rhodolite Garnet, Sardonyx, Shiva Lingam, Snakeskin & Red & Brown Agate, Tangerine Quartz, Thulite

    This Chakra is the center of your creative and sexual expression. The creative dynamics in your immediate environment leave an energy imprint on this Chakra in the second year of your life. This plays a crucial part in your self-identification process. You create your persona by way of individual expression and identify with your personal and physical relationships, which can either spiritually elevate you, or bring you down into the entrapments of Earthly desires. Second Chakra can be challenging when striving for inner harmony and peace. Today's society pressures us to fit into a specific category, which none of us do. Each person is very unique and it is important to remember your true authentic Soul essence. A harmonious environment that supports your free creative expression holds the key.

> **YOUR CREATIVITY IS ESSENTIAL FOR YOUR INNER BALANCE, FULFILLMENT OF DESIRES AND REALIZATION OF YOUR DREAMS. EXPRESS YOURSELF WITH YOUR BODY, MIND, HEART AND SOUL.**

    If you do not find a proper channel for your creative force, it will negatively affect all your upper Chakras, specifically the Fifth. This can result in upset verbal expression, either saying things you don't mean, or excessive chatter. If your creativity is channeled in a healthy way, your speech will flow smoothly and with ease. The process of self-identification is not an easy one to master. Ignoring issues of this Chakra will have overwhelming repercussions that may affect every area of your life. By healing them you will attract harmony and accelerate your ascension. Your artistic and sexual expression help you feel alive and in touch with your deepest inner makings. The ultimate creativity originates from your Soul. In an evolved physical interaction, two Souls unite lovingly and equally, absent of manipulation or competition. All creative endeavors require bravery. When you express your true self, you open up to the possibility of rejection, criticism or denial. But you also open up to experience the ultimate unconditional love, acceptance, praise and genuine admiration.

    Do you carry enough courage? Life is full of choices and unpredictable surprises. To live fully requires the audacity to take a chance. Only so will you eventually experience what you desire and long for, your freedom of creative expression, great communication, unconditional love and acceptance. Find that finely tuned and delicate balance with the help of this Mudra.

MUDRA FOR CHAKRA II.

Sit with a straight back, keep your shoulders down, nice and relaxed. Place a Crystal in your hands and let it rest between the two palms, or you may place a small Crystals in each hand. Now lift your hands up to level just below the throat. Cup your hands with palms up, fingers pointing up. The thumbs and pinkies are outstretched, while the other three fingers are held together. The sides of little fingers and base of your palms are touching. Thumbs are pointing toward your body. Hold for three minutes and relax.

BREATH
LONG, DEEP AND SLOW THRU YOUR NOSE
MANTRA
SAT NAM (*Truth Is God's Name, One in Spirit*)
AFFIRMATION
MY CREATIVE FORCE IS IN PERFECT BALANCE

MUDRAS and CRYSTALS ~ by SABRINA MESKO ~ 79

Third Chakra

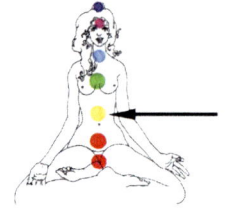

REPRESENTS: Ego, emotional center, the intellect, the mind
LOCATION: Solar plexus **COLOR:** Yellow **AROMA:** Sage **KEY AGE:** 3
DESIRES: Immortality, authority, fame, recognition, power, adoration, praise, stardom
CHALLENGES: Pride, vanity, control, aggression, competing, tyranny, selfishness, bullying

CRYSTALS: Adamite, Ametrine, Citrine, Desert Rose, Desirite, Golden Beryl, Golden Calcite, Golden Herkimer, Golden Quartz, Moonstone, Peridot, Pumice, Tiger Iron, Tiger's Eye, Yellow Apatite, Yellow Jade, Yellow Jasper, Yellow Topaz, Yellow Tourmaline, Youngite

This Chakra is the center of your ego and the mind. The interpersonal dynamics of control leave an energy imprint on this Chakra in the third year of your life. Ego is the ever powerful force that is always resisting, opposing and battling with your heart. This is where your ego makes the last ditch effort to keep you stuck in the lower frequency realms while provoking the challenging emotions of fear, the main obstacle on your ascension journey. This Chakra also holds your anger, which is an unexpressed, unfulfilled and desperate scream for love and attention. Once you overcome this entrapment, you are on your way to spiritual freedom. Your mind holds the key to overcoming these negative character traits. You can make a conscious decision to overcome bad patterns, and strive for a deeper understanding of your spiritual purpose. Find a balance while listening to both - your mind and heart. Ego and intellect may find the perfect reason why you dreams are impractical, but your heart will guide you to their fulfillment.

**OVERCOMING FEAR AND EGO WILL REQUIRE COURAGE AND SACRIFICE.
BUT THE REWARDS WILL BE INDESCRIBABLY BEAUTIFUL,
THE STUFF THAT DREAMS ARE MADE OF...
YOU'LL AWAKEN YOUR HEART AND ENTER THE REALM OF TRUE LOVE.**

We all have an ego, and it usually has something to say, whether we like it or not. But your ego can be balanced and under control if you keep a clear perspective on higher principles. When you truly understand and accept the fleeting glory of the worldly success resulting from purely self-centered motivation, you will learn to discern who or what rules your life. You will overcome the earthly entrapments and open your mind. Your ego will be present, but it won't rule your life. Understanding your ego will help you understand others who may also struggle with this issue. You won't judge them, but will strive to inspire and help them instead.

Managing the limitations and complexities of the ego will help you learn about compassion and kindness. It is the strength of your character that holds the reigns of your ego. This can be your rulebook, so you become the master of your wondrous mind. Always listen to your heart, for it is only your love that becomes etched in the Universal records of eternity. This Mudra is very effective in helping you master and remain in charge of your mind and your choices.

MUDRA FOR STRONG CHARACTER

Sit with a straight back, shoulders down, nice and relaxed. Place a Wand Crystal in each hand, and hold your hands in relaxed fists, tips of Crystals aligned with your straight index fingers. Thumbs are on the outside of the fist, regardless of the Crystal size. Lift the right hand higher, closer to your mind, calling for mind-ego balance. Your left hand, connected to your heart is lower, closer to your heart. Palms are facing each other. Index fingers are pointing up, towards the sky. Absorb the power of each Crystal as it channels energy through its tip. Focus on the clarity of mind and intention. Practice for three minutes.

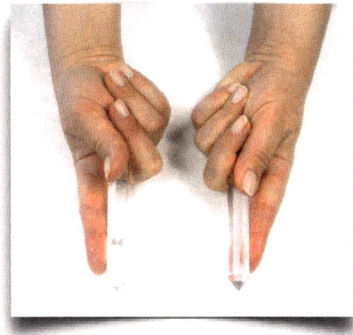

BREATH
LONG, DEEP AND SLOW THRU YOUR NOSE

MANTRA
HUMME HUM BRAHAM *(Calling on the Infinite Self)*

AFFIRMATION
I AM THE MASTER OF MY MIND

CROSSING OVER

This is a major milestone. The moment you actually manage to ascend and elevate your essential frequency into the harmonious zone of the heart, everything shifts. You are at a beautiful and critical point in your evolutionary process. You overcame tremendous challenges and seductive obstacles, and you learned and recognized the truth within the ultimate truth:

> **THE ONLY ANSWER TO UNDERSTAND, EMBRACE AND ACCEPT IS LOVE.**
> **LIVE YOUR LIFE WITH LOVE, THRU LOVE AND IN LOVE.**
> **COMPASSION, KINDNESS, GRACE AND FORGIVENESS RESIDE IN LOVE.**
> **LOVE IS THE ANSWER YOU ARE SEEKING.**

If you want to be free of past burdens you need to forgive and move on. Only the ability to do so with love is a worthy option. Of course this may seem much more difficult at the time. It is considerably easier to get reactive, explode with anger and fury, than calm down and emit unwavering love. This is especially true when you face the raw nature of the "human animal" in its harshest form. But if you react to anyone with negative emotions of hate, anger and revenge, you are no better than them. You have been pulled into their spinning negative abyss, which is hard to escape. As a result, your frequency will descends and function in a lower field. To overcome the most challenging human weakness, the desire to get even, make a choice to trust in Universal rule of law. Nothing escapes it, for there are no exceptions.

Functioning on the higher frequency level does not make you immune to occasional descent into the darkness of lower realms. Actually, there is a specific occasion that could pull you into this direction, when you feel genuine love for another human being, who may be more comfortable on the lower Chakra level.

As I mentioned previously, if one partner functions at the third or lower Chakra level and the other partner naturally vibrates at the fourth or higher Chakra level, the only possibility for a deep connection will be when the more evolved partner sacrifices their own natural state and embarks on a necessary descent. Yes, the lower person's frequency will temporarily rise, purely because love will uplift them, but sooner or later, they will return to their natural lower frequency. This can be very challenging and may create suffering and conflict. However, by using and working with Crystals, you can truly help maintain your natural Fourth Chakra or higher level, even while enduring unharmonious dynamics with others. This can be of immense help.

If you find yourself in a relationship that is energetically challenging, you can program a Crystal to help you remain stable and return to your natural frequency level. This Crystal will be indeed your anchor to prevent you from descending so low, that you endure suffering and unnecessary pain and hurt. It will also help you understand, that it is in your best interest to pursue and attract relationships on your level of energetic compatibility. You may have to experience a challenging relationship where the energy frequency unity will be an issue, but a Crystal will help you process and journey thru the experience faster and safer.

Remember, the Crystal functions at a high frequency level and is a most reliable fine energy being that never fluctuates. It is as stable and secure as you can imagine. Once your general frequency is stabilized in the Fourth Chakra, the natural progression continues in its time. Working with Crystals will help you progress faster and avoid unnecessary repetition of destructive patterns. Keep in mind, that your natural functioning at heart Chakra level does not necessarily mean you have mastered all its challenges. Until you are able to love unconditionally as well as equally give and receive love, you will remain on that level. Each time you progress to the next frequency level, your soul experiences profound changes. You are quite aware of your awakening ascension process and eventually become self-realized.

THE PROCESS of ASCENSION

The clearest indication that your cellular and subtle energy structure is shifting frequencies, is revealed by your changed reaction to outside stimuli and shift in your actions and desires. If you have unresolved attachments connected to the first three Chakras, they will remain in your ethereal body, even if you try to convince yourself otherwise. Unexpectedly, a trigger will happen and force you to face issues you thought were resolved, but are in fact not.

It is almost like working thru an addiction, where numbing and ignoring challenging habits is the farthest thing from a viable solution. The best cleansing and balancing technique is to face your innermost desires and try to understand them from the physical, mental, emotional and spiritual perspectives. Ask yourself what are your deficiencies in each of these areas that cause you to continue an unhealthy habit. If you do not find a clear answer, it's time to look deeper. A cause may reside in your being as a considerably older memory than you may consciously remember. One way to recall events from your deeper past is a spontaneous past life regression, which can occur in deep states of meditation. The purpose of such immersion work is to help clear the obstructed pathways and establish your inner peace. Your eventual ascension is the destined purpose of your human experience.

When you overcome the entrapment of the Third Chakra, you move steadily further into the Fourth Chakra of unconditional love, the Fifth chakra of speaking the ultimate and inspiring truth, the Sixth Chakra of absolute inner attunement, and finally the Seventh Chakra of Divine awareness and illumination, where you lastly merge with the source of it all, the infinite Light. This is your Soul's evolutionary process on this plane of limited dimensional existence. Once we have mastered this plane, there are numerous other planes of existence that we experience next. What matters most in our very limited ability to understand this concept, is to focus on where we are at this very moment in time. You are here. It is always constructive to have an open mind about the field of endless possibilities. Now we continue on this fascinating journey through the upper Chakras. The gates of mystery shall open wide and reveal most wondrous discoveries.

Crystal Chakra Wand

Fourth Chakra

REPRESENTS: Unconditional true love, devotion, faith, compassion, kindness
LOCATION: Heart **COLOR:** Green and pink **AROMA:** Rose **KEY AGE:** 4
DESIRES: Love, faith, devotion, duty
ACQUIRED DISTINCTIONS: Harmony within inner and outer world, happy, youthful, aware of life's actions and karma, striving to achieve balance, clarity of conscience

CRYSTALS: Actinolite, Aventurine, Charoite, Chrysoprase, Emerald, Epidote, Fluorite, Green Quartz, Green Sapphire, Jet, Kunzite, Lavender Quartz, Magnesite, Malachite, Opal, Peridot, Pink & Green Tourmaline, Quartz, Rainbow & Green Obsidian, Rhodochritem, Rose Quartz, Uvarovite Garnet

This Chakra is your Heart. Many of us go thru phases in our lives where our heart seems almost dormant, as if sleeping. This may be a consequence of a painful heartbreak, or clear denial of our feelings. Perhaps you are busy with distractions and other life events and simply forget to pay attention to your heart's needs. But eventually something occurs that breaks your shell and cracks you wide open. And it is thru these circumstances that your heart awakens. A metamorphosis occurs, you feel transformed and alive with the power of love. This very personal process may take time and require patience.

Your heart's receptivity to love is determined at an early age. The lower three Chakras are energetically set and firmed up in the first three years of your life, and your heart is most delicate and receptive at age four. The interpretation and demonstration of love until or at that time, will leave an energy imprint on this Chakra and affect your future romantic relationships and partners you choose. Relationships are ideal opportunities for growth, self-realization, and spiritual ascension. There is no logic or reasoning when it comes to true love. It is an incredibly complex and intricate dynamic, that involves karma and previous soul contracts. All relationships require conscious effort to keep the connection healthy and vibrant. It is important to develop your ability for self-love and maintain an uplifted heart. This is a prerequisite for attracting a compatible partner. Paying attention to your heart is essential.

> ### THE LOVE STORY OF YOUR HEART IS ETERNAL.
> ### IT GOES ON UNTIL YOUR LAST BREATH AND BEYOND.
> ### NEVER DOUBT THAT LOVE WILL FIND YOU, FOR YOU ARE LOVE ITSELF.

The search for love is an ongoing mission whether we admit it or not. It is most important to fully believe that you deserve and shall receive love in your life. Anything that is blocking and preventing love from entering your life must be released and let go. A loving pet can be a most heart-healing ally. Cultivate love towards yourself and others, and you will attract and receive love in such abundance, it will overwhelm you. This Mudra is a power tool for harmonizing your heart center and attracting kindred spirits, with perfectly paired intentions.

MUDRA FOR CHAKRA IV.

Sit with a straight back, keep your shoulders down, nice and relaxed. Place a Crystal of choice in each hand. Lift your right hand up, elbow bent, your hand at the level of your face. Make a fist and leave only the index finger extended, pointing up. If you are using a Crystal Wand, it must be pointed towards the sky. Place your left hand on your chest above your breast, elbow parallel to the ground. Gently hold the Crystal against your chest and feel your heart open and merge with the healing energy of the Crystal. Keep the elbows nice and high. Visualize the uplifting energy shift in your body. Practice for three minutes.

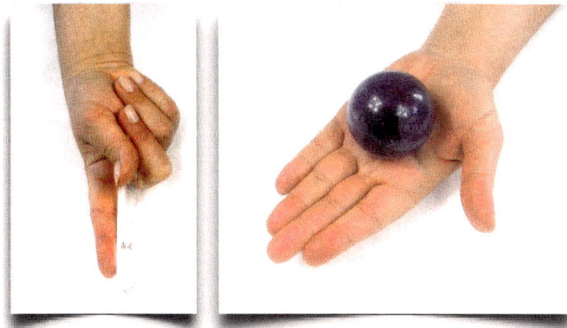

BREATH
LONG, DEEP AND SLOW THRU YOUR NOSE

MANTRA
SAT NAM (*Truth is God's name, One in Spirit*)

AFFIRMATION
MY HEART IS OPEN AND BEAMING WITH LOVE

Fifth Chakra

REPRESENTS: Voice, truth, communication, higher knowledge
LOCATION: Throat **COLOR:** Blue **AROMA:** Geranium **KEY AGE:** 5
DESIRE: Knowledge, truth, communicating through inspiration
ACQUIRED DISTINCTIONS: Distracting nature of the Earthly realm is no longer a challenge, gained ability for supreme reasoning, seeks truth, honesty, purity

CRYSTALS: Angelite, Aquamarine, Barite, Blue Lace Agate, Blue Obsidian, Blue Phantom Quartz, Blue Quartz, Blue Spinel, Blue Topaz, Blue Tourmaline, Celestite, Indicolite Quartz, Lapis Lazuli, Quartz, Sapphire, Sodalite, Turquoise

This Chakra governs your voice of truth. The speaking dynamics you've witnessed and learned until or at age five, will leave a strong energy imprint on this Chakra at that time. Functioning at the Fifth Chakra level grants you access to higher knowledge and an ability to speak in a most uplifting and inspiring manner. If you believe you are already vibrating at the level of fifth Chakra, you most likely still need to develop further. In order for you to vibrate at that frequency level, it would require an absolute absence of Earthly desires in your heart, body and mind. You would need to master supreme ability for detachment, reasoning, and be entirely immune to any weakness of your ego. That is a high aspiration.

WHEN LIVING IN THE FIFTH CHAKRA FREQUENCY STATE YOU INSPIRE OTHERS WITH WORDS OF WISDOM AND KINDNESS. YOU STAND BY TRUTH, REGARDLESS OF CONSEQUENCES. YOU ARE THE MESSENGER OF PEACE.

Mudras and selected Crystals will greatly help empower and activate your Fifth Chakra, so that you may express yourself for who you truly are, and master a most uplifting and harmonious transmission of your intended message. Your ability to communicate is a crucial tool in your life. And quite often many hurtful, unhappy and unhealthy situations could be entirely prevented with truthful and kind conversation. It is important to examine your own ability to interact, or tendency to avoid speaking up. When intending to voice your needs or desires, your silence is most counterproductive. You can't expect others to guess your wishes, thoughts and opinions. By doing so, you are actually giving away your power, while waiting for others to determine your future. Certainly at times it may seem very difficult to find the courage to speak up. By adding a powerful Mudra and Crystal activating jolt to your Fifth Chakra, you will gain the ability to convey what you need, in order to accomplish your optimal desired results. Your voice is your clear message to the world about who you are, what you wish, need and want. This Mudra will help you evoke, empower and clarify your ability to communicate. The effects will magnify with the use of your Crystal, so that you may speak with crystal clarity and efficiency.

MUDRA FOR CHAKRA V.

Sit with a straight back, keep your shoulders down, nice and relaxed. Place a Crystal of choice in each hand. Bend your elbows, lifting them up parallel to the ground. Make fists with both hands, leaving the index fingers pointing straight up. If you are using Crystal Wands, they must be pointed towards the sky. Bring your hands up to either side of your head, palms facing towards you. Hold and be aware of the Crystal energy magnifying your overall energy field and charging your hands and fingers. Your confidence for speaking up is activated while perfectly balanced. Practice for three minutes.

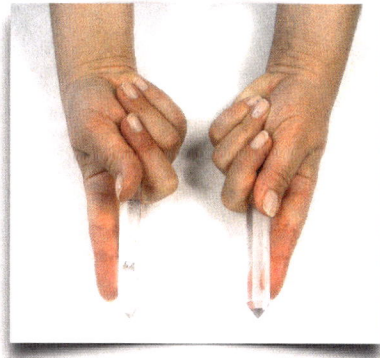

BREATH
LONG, DEEP AND SLOW THRU YOUR NOSE

MANTRA
EK ONG KAR *(One Creator, God Is One)*

AFFIRMATION
I EXPRESS MY TRUTH WITH GREAT CLARITY

Sixth Chakra

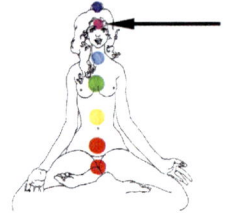

REPRESENTS: Third Eye, vision, intuition, Divine wisdom
LOCATION: Third Eye **COLOR**: Indigo **AROMA:** Sandalwood **KEY AGE:** 6
ACQUIRED DISTINCTIONS: Ability to perceive visions from past, present and future, clear perception, spiritual decline not probable, a sense of duality is dissolved

CRYSTALS: Agrellite, Amethyst, Ammolite, Angelite, Annabergite, Aquamarine, Blue Halite, Azurite, Blue & Green Opal, Blue & Lavender & White Jade, Blue Agate, Blue Aragonite, Blue Fluorite, Blue Obsidian, Blue Selenite, Blue Topaz, Blue-green Jade, Bornite, Chrysolite, Clear & Rhomboid Calcite, Datolite, Green Calcite, Green Selenite, Herkimer Diamond, Howlite, Iolite, Lapis Lazuli, Molybdenite, Moonstone, Ocean Jasper, Pietersite, Seraphina, Serpentine, Sodolite, Moonstone, Star-seed & Candle & Fenster & Sichuan Quartz, Sugilite, Tanzanite, Ulexite

   This Chakra is your window into infinity. The individual ability to naturally follow your intuition will leave an energy imprint on this Chakra at age six. We all want to know the future, easily discern challenging situations, perceive the true nature of everyone we meet and find the answers to most pressing questions. The ability to use your intuition at will can be developed with diligent and dedicated practice. Activating this Chakra demands conscious effort and concentration in order to "pry open" your Third Eye window that may offer you a glimpse into the realms of higher knowledge. This invisible, unknown world holds all the answers you are searching for at one time or another. But the more desperate you become, the more unreliable and evasive your connection becomes. Learn patience and discipline.

> **WHEN STRIVING TO OPEN YOUR THIRD EYE
> CULTIVATE A CALM STATE OF INNER PERCEPTION.
> THE UNIVERSAL KNOWLEDGE IS WITHIN YOUR REACH.**

   If you are healing practitioner, the access to your intuition is your essential tool. When it comes to truly mastering your insight, you need to begin with a realistic perception of yourself. You are the most complex puzzle to solve, before you tackle solving others. Otherwise you run the danger of projecting your own confusion, misconception and unfulfilled desires onto someone else's personal situation. In any case, you must learn to balance your personal challenges, so that they won't in any way hinder or affect your ability to discern. A well developed intuition is a wondrous gift, a supreme navigation system that helps you avoid undesirable experiences and propels you towards fulfilling your life mission. It is indescribably fascinating and truly priceless. This powerful Mudra practiced with Crystals will help open up your Third Eye, so that you may gain clear vision and expand the perception of the past, present and the future.

Mudra for Chakra VI.

Sit with a straight back, keep your shoulders down, nice and relaxed. Place a Crystal in each hand. Select smaller Crystals that can fit and be easily held in area between your thumb and the index finger, touching the palm area under the index. The area between the thumb and the index finger is called the first thenar webspace. Bend your elbows and lift your arms up to so that the elbows are parallel to the ground. Palms are facing out and all fingers are together. Hold for three minutes and concentrate on your Third Eye.

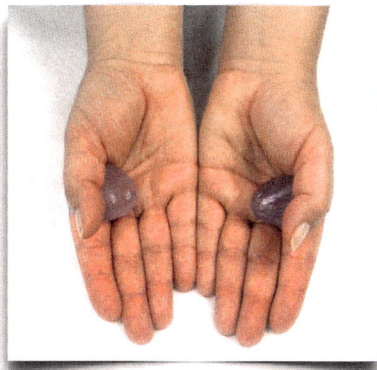

BREATH
LONG, DEEP AND SLOW THRU YOUR NOSE

MANTRA
EK ONG KAR *(One Creator, God Is One)*

AFFIRMATION
I SEE THROUGH THE WINDOW OF INFINITY

Seventh Chakra

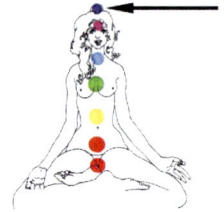

REPRESENTS: Universal God consciousness, the heavens, unity, humility
LOCATION: Crown **COLOR:** Violet **AROMA:** Lavender **KEY AGE:** 7
ACQUIRED DISTINCTIONS: All feelings, emotions and desires are diffused, attainable state of Samadhi, pure bliss and unity

CRYSTALS: Amethyst, Angel's Wing, Apophyllite, Aqua Aura Quartz, Azaztulite, Azurite, Blue Selenite, Botswana Agate, Cat's Eye, Cathedral & Celestial & Faden & Spirit Quartz, Celestite, Charoite, Clear Beryl, Clear Topaz, Colorless Tourmaline, Cymophane, Diamond, Drusy Chrysocolla, Gem Silica, Halite, Labradorite, Lapis Lazuli, Lavender Jade, Lilac Kunzite, Novaculite, Petalite, Phenacite, Purple Jasper, Purple Sapphire, Purpurite, Selenite, Silver Sheen Obsidian, White Jade, White Sapphire

This Chakra commands your trust in unity with Divine Universal Power. A natural ability to trust and recognize Divine presence will create an energy imprint on this Chakra at age seven. It is an inevitable fact of life that we will experience suffering. But upon deeper reflection there is always a silver lining, a much needed lesson, experience or sacrifice that we must endure in order to advance in our evolutionary process. The big picture is intricately more complex than we could ever imagine. Your unwavering trust will play a crucial role in how you endure and eventually survive various obstacles throughout your life. Your effectiveness depends on your ability to call upon the Universe and hear its guidance. When life presents you with challenges, gather your strength, rise above it all and proclaim: "I trust that I am Divinely protected, for the Universe loves me and guides me in the best way possible."

CALL UPON YOUR SPIRIT GUIDES.
BELIEVE AND TRUST IN THE UNIVERSE AND DIVINE GUARDIANSHIP.
YOUR INNER FLAME IS ETERNALLY CONNECTED TO THE LIGHT.

Using Crystal power when working on this Chakra field will expand your inner force, activate your ability to connect with, and magnify your higher awareness. By raising your frequency, you will be closer to finer, subtle field of information and higher consciousness and will develop a clear dialogue between the "Earthly you" and your higher self, so that you will never feel abandoned or lost. Trusting the Universe allows wonderful opportunities to come to life, so that you may experience all you desire and more.

We learn most valuable lessons and recognize our life purpose while going thru the darkest nigh of our soul. An unexpected revelation will pry open the invisible door so you may enter into another world, where love and Light prevail. This powerful Mudra practiced with a Crystal will help you hold a strong field of trust in knowing everything is happening precisely as it should, and you are loved and protected beyond measure. Your humble request for help was heard. Trust that the guiding answer will emerge at a predestined moment in time.

MUDRA FOR TRUST

Sit with a straight back and keep your shoulders down, nice and relaxed. Take a Crystal into your right hand and place it over the back of the left hand. The Crystal is held in the space between hands. Lift your arms up, stretched up and above your head, creating a circle. Press the thumb tips together and visualize a protective circle of white light surrounding you. Now tune into the power of the Crystal and magnify this power tenfold. Hold this energy strong and unwavering in your mind and sense a soothing calmness overcome your entire being. Trust that you shielded in the field of Universal protection. Practice for three minutes. Men hold a reversed position, the left palm on top of right.

BREATH
FAST, SHORT BREATH OF FIRE FROM NAVEL

MANTRA
HAR HAR HAR WAHE GURU *(God's Creation, His supreme power and Wisdom)*

AFFIRMATION
I TRUST THE UNIVERSE LOVES AND PROTECTS ME

CRYSTAL GAZING

After your Mudra practice, spend some time in deep meditation with your Crystal. This is the perfect moment to explore Crystal gazing, while observing it in a relaxed, calm and contemplative state. In the past this kind of gazing was used with Crystal spheres, but it can be done with any kind of a clear Crystal that contains structures and unusual shades, visible yet untouchable to human hands. A Crystal has an outer body as well as a mysterious interior. Most of the time, you can actually see this interior Crystal universe. In fact, it is incredibly mesmerizing and quite astonishing.

The easiest way to observe the interior is with a clear quartz Crystal. You can see phantoms, mirrors, rainbows and truly cosmic-like formations and structures that project an air of infinity and otherworldly mystery. You can't see everything, but if you really know how to observe, you will discover sights you never imagined. Unusual objects, shades and reflections that will transform and take you into another world, where you have access to higher knowledge. You may unexpectedly understand a hidden message, an important vision, or a clear sentence. Perhaps an answer may suddenly appear in your mind. This is one of Crystal's many sacred powers.

To help you understand the depth and complexity of Crystal interior, observe this example of magnified interior structures. When you arrive at a point of complete stillness and receptivity, you can actually communicate with Crystal's essence and understand certain information that may be helpful to you at this particular moment. The fascination with a Crystal never ends, because it hides so many incredible messages that you may not notice in the beginning, but with time, they become clearer and more pronounced. Explore Crystal gazing and notice the different state of consciousness and receptivity you will experience. Pay attention to any other surprising messages you'll receive from your new ally.

The Marvels inside the Mysterious World of Smoky Citrine

Chapter Seven

Mudras & Crystals

PHYSICAL PROTECTION SHIELD

Mudra for Recharging with Amethyst Sphere

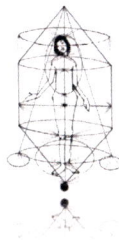

Your Body is Your Vehicle

Your body is a natural marvel that serves you in order to experience life as a human being on this Earthly realm. As a finely tuned machine with incredible capacities, your body is programmed to survive and go on as long as possible, while adjusting, regenerating, adapting and transforming in most amazing ways. We only see the outer shell of our physical body, but our finer, subtle energy layers absorb all frequencies that we are exposed to. With time, the consequences of unhealthy lifestyle, unharmonious relationships, negative mindset, unresolved emotions, chronically depleted energy states and ongoing disharmony can develop into a physical challenge or illness. To prevent this from occurring, we need to lead a healthy and vibrant life in a loving, safe and nurturing environment, free of toxins and stress. To help protect ourselves from challenging environmental frequency elements, we require a highly resilient energy shield that remains undetected on the physical level, yet works on subtle realms, preventing unharmonious frequencies from penetrating our energy body and causing harm.

As we know, Crystals have been used by various cultures for protection and help when warding off negative energies. They easily maintain a high frequency environment that is impossible to alter or reduce to lower frequencies. However, this does not in any way suggest that one can blindly rely only on Crystals for protection. Your state of wellness requires your conscious participation and effort. You need to be aware of your environment, the people in it, your actions and choices that ultimately determine your overall health and safety. If you live with a sense of awareness, your positive intentions, behavior and choices will make a crucial difference. Crystals can greatly assist you in this effort and help you establish a solid and unwavering protective energy shield.

To make this process most effective, your personal preparation is of utter importance. The first step requires a subtle energy cleansing, by having a clear intention to release any negative thoughts, projections, emotions and stagnant energy states you may carry in your deep subconscious mind. If you attempt to create and energy protection shield prematurely, your protection will not be as effective. For example, if you are fearful, you need to have an intention to release your fear, before sealing-off your protective Aura shield. You intention will clarify your desired new healthy mindset pattern and your Crystal will help you manifest and fortify that intention.

In order to successfully establish your subtle protective shield, the first and foremost requirement is to take great care of your outer layer - your physical body. The basic steps are a healthy lifestyle, proper food and nutrition for your body's specific needs, enough rest and sleep, physical movement, healthy breathing for proper oxygenation, and elimination of any destructive habits or toxic substances that directly harm your physical body. Each one of these aspects is of great importance. Nutrition is increasingly more complex because of all the toxic substances that are found in various foods. You can not expect that all organic food is the ideal diet for your physical constitution. Discovering which foods agree and disagree with your unique needs is a necessity. Food that inflames your digestive tract and consequently your brain is to be avoided at all cost.

Halite

Food allergies are very common and can be brought under control with the help of elimination diet. This requires patience and discipline. Create a very basic menu and see how you feel. Then slowly add new foods each week and pay close attention to any changes. A single food item that does not agree with you could disrupt your delicate inner balance. In addition, any self-destructive or addictive tendencies such as excessive use of alcohol, mind altering drugs or smoking, will weaken your subtle energy body, making it vulnerable to external negative influences. If you are mentally and emotionally depleted and don't distance yourself from a negative environment or people, you are contributing to your deterioration. When you are unaware of your overall weakened state, you will subconsciously attract energies that will feed on your vulnerability and energy deficiency. Self-awareness and taking responsibility for your thoughts, actions, projections, choices and decisions is of greatest importance.

Functioning in fear considerably lowers your overall frequency, while functioning in love uplifts and raises your frequency. Therefore it is most important to establish a state of fearlessness and love. This is necessary in order to help sustain a resilient energy shield for your overall protection. Fear on any level will affect your ability to connect and trust in Divine protection. Remember, you are a complex multi-dimensional being, yet interconnected into ONE living presence. With a conscious intention to strengthen your emotional, mental and physical disposition, you will be able to create and sustain a subtle protection shield that will envelop all your energy body layers.

> **YOUR AIM IS TO BECOME PHYSICALLY STRONG, MENTALLY CONFIDENT, EMOTIONALLY BALANCED AND SPIRITUALLY ATTUNED.**

With the Mudras presented in this chapter, the intention and focus is on establishing, strengthening and preserving the balance and harmony of your physical body. After you have completed the basic steps of preparing your Crystal, you are ready to begin your practice. Visualize a great ball of white light. See it emitting from your Crystal and entirely surrounding you in a beautiful glow of pure impenetrable Light. Maintaining this visualization during your Mudra and Crystal practice will help you establish an unwavering protection shield to help withstand any disturbance or negative energy directed at you personally, by intention or mere environmental circumstance. The moment you sense self-doubt or fear, your energy field becomes weaker, more accessible and vulnerable. Keep disciplined and persistent in your practice and with time you will establish an incredibly efficient, solid, reliable and indestructible shield of protection. Maintain it with love and care.

On the next page, you will find a list of Crystals that carry protective frequencies and are ideal for helping you establish a high frequency protective shield. Since various Crystals offer a wide array of benefits, use your intuition in determining which particular Crystal is ideal for your needs. Any Crystal that you have programed for a specific purpose can be also used for creating a strong protective energy shield.

Red Jasper with Quartz

CRYSTALS WITH POWERFUL PROTECTIVE ENERGIES

All Crystals offer countless benefits. This list specifies the most potent Crystals for use with Mudras when creating an Energy Protective Shield for your Body, Mind, Heart and Astral subtle field.

AGATE - ancient Roman amulet for protection, helps with self confidence, Aura stability

AMBER - helps establish great protective shield for healers, prevents energy vampirism

APACHE TEAR - offers excellent protection and absorbs negative energy

AVENTURINE - holds a protective grid, clears electromagnetic smog, mind & heart balance

BERYL - protection from outside influences & manipulation, aids with stress, re-awakens love

BLACK OBSIDIAN - immediate protection against negativity, blocks psychic attacks

BLACK TOURMALINE - blocks psychic attacks & electromagnetic and negative energies

BLUE HALITE - guards from negative energies, entity attachment & attack

CALCEDONY - guards from accidents & psychic attacks, dissipates negativity, clears illness

CARNELIAN - ancient Egyptian protective stone, removes fear of death, attracts abundance

CAT'S EYE - ancient Assyrian stone of invisibility, protection, dispels negativity

CITRINE - transmutes negativity, reverses self-destructiveness, mental protector

EMERALD - physical and mental protection, clarity, discernment, mental balance & love

FLUORITE - blocks electromagnetic stress & negativity, stabilizes aura, heightens intuition

HEMATITE - protects aura during out of body experiences, heals and balances body and spirit

HERKIMER DIAMOND - excellent Soul shield, electromagnetic cleaner, activates Light body

JADE - offers strong protection, can undo physical harm, great for stabilizing mind and body

JASPER - physical protection from pollution, aligns physical, mental, emotional & ethereal realms

JET - ancient magical talisman against dark entities, protects from illness, alleviates fear

LABRADORITE - protective, deflects negative energies, removes hooks in your aura

LAPIS LAZULI - ancient Egyptian stone for alerts & protection from attacks, empowers telepathy

MAGNETITE - strong magnetic powers, it helps remove you from danger, promotes grounding

MALACHITE - offers protection against negative spirits, absorbs pollutants, heals the Earth

MOOKAITE JASPER - helps to remain calm and make choices during challenges, see also Jasper

MOONSTONE - protects from overwhelming emotion, strengthens inner balance, clairvoyance

PERIDOT - keeps away negative energies, protects aura, cleanser, purifies, helps letting go

PREHNITE - seals the auric field in a protective shield, connecting to the Universe's energy grid

PYRITE - excellent energy shield, blocks negative energy, deflects harm

RAINBOW OBSIDIAN - strong aura protection, helps cut love cords, energy hooks in heart

RUBY - ancient Vedic protector, shields against psychic attacks & vampirism of heart energy

RUTILATED QUARTZ - guards from psychic attacks, releases fears, facilitates healing & change

SAPPHIRE - Vedic healing stone of wisdom, fights negative forces, releases negative thoughts

SELENITE - angelic consciousness, anchors Light body, protective grid, grasp of subconscious

SERPENTINE - protects against toxins, parasites elimination, mental & emotional balance

SULFUR - drives off negativity, karmic cleansing, absorbs destructiveness, removes barriers

SUNSTONE - assists in fulfilling karmic contracts, removes energy hooks, cuts energy ties

TIGER's EYE - energy of Sun and Earth, strong protective field, creates high vibrational state

TOPAZ - promotes trust in Universe, balances emotions, aligns body's meridians, cleans aura

TREE AGATE - protection against negativity, aura stabilization, see also Agate

TURQUOISE - Native American protector against injury, outside forces, pollutants, self-sabotage

WATERMELON TOURMALINE - balances chakras, creates protective shield, transform density into lighter frequencies, mental healer, extremely beneficial for wounded healers

ZICRON - protection against robbers, lightning, body harm, disease, energy body balance

MUDRA FOR DEVELOPING MEDITATION

Sit with a straight back and keep your shoulders down, nice and relaxed. Place a small Crystal in the palm of your left hand. Hold it open and facing the sky. Lift up your hands to the level of solar plexus and place the four fingers of the right hand on your left wrist to feel your pulse. Pressing lightly, the fingers of the right hand are positioned nicely in a straight line on the wrist of the left hand. Concentrate and completely focus on your pulse. Hands and elbows are away from body. With each pulse-beat, repeat the mantra Sat Nam. After a minute, practice without mantra and expand your awareness to connect with the Universal heartbeat. Continue for Three minutes and relax.

BREATH
LONG, DEEP AND SLOW THRU YOUR NOSE
MANTRA
SAT NAM (*Truth is God's name, One in Spirit*)
AFFIRMATION
I AM ONE WITH THE UNIVERSE

Mudra for Physical Protection

Sit with a straight back, shoulders down, nice and relaxed. Take a Crystal into each hand. Place both hands on your upper chest, and cross your left hand over the right one. Crystals are resting between your hands and your chest. Palms are facing you and all fingers are together. Focus on the healing power from your hands magnified by the power of the Crystals. Hold for Three minutes.

BREATH
LONG, DEEP AND SLOW THRU YOUR NOSE
MANTRA
OM *(God in His Absolute State)*
AFFIRMATION
THE DIVINE LIGHT IS MY EVERLASTING PROTECTOR

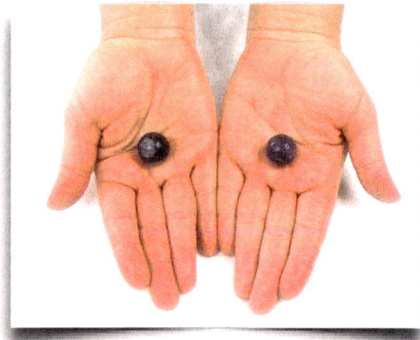

Mudra for Protecting Your Health

    Sit with a straight back, shoulders down, nice and relaxed. Place a small Crystal in the palm of each hand. Bend your right elbow and lift your hand up, palm facing forward. The index and middle fingers are pointing up; the rest are curled with the thumb over, while holding the Crystal. Hold your left hand in the same Mudra with the outstretched index and middle finger touching your heart. Hold for three minutes and relax.

BREATH
INHALE FOR TEN COUNTS, HOLD THE BREATH FOR TEN COUNTS,
AND EXHALE FOR TEN COUNTS

MANTRA
OM *(God in His Absolute State)*

AFFIRMATION
I AM VIBRANT WITH HEALTH

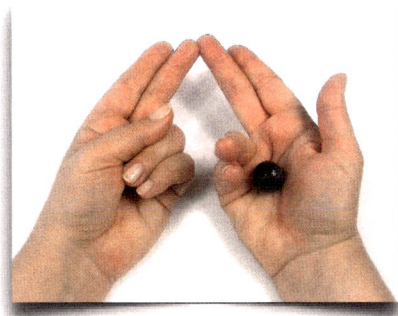

MUDRA FOR PREVENTING BURNOUT

Sit with a straight back, shoulders down, nice and relaxed. Place a small Crystal in each hand and with your hands slightly cupped, lightly fold your thumbs over the small Crystals to keep them in place. Bring your forearms up in front of you at heart level and bend your elbows to the side, palms facing down towards the ground, all fingers together. Now slightly curve your fingers and touch your middle finger tips, forming a V-shape with your hands. Your elbows remain elevated. Hold for three minutes and relax.

BREATH
LONG, DEEP AND SLOW THRU YOUR NOSE
MANTRA
OM *(God in His Absolute State)*
AFFIRMATION
MY ENERGY FIELD IS SELF-SUSTAINED

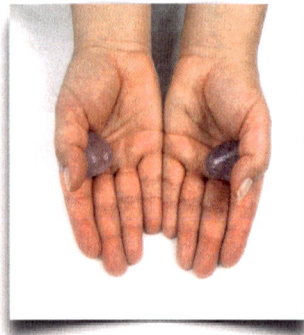

MUDRA FOR RECHARGING

Sit with a straight back, shoulders down, nice and relaxed. Place a Crystal in the palm of your right hand and hold it in a fist. Extend your arms in front of you, parallel to the ground, keeping your elbows straight. Wrap the left hand around the right hand. The bases of the palms are touching. Both thumbs are outstretched, touching alongside and pointing straight up. Hold for three minutes and relax.

BREATH
LONG, DEEP AND SLOW THRU YOUR NOSE

AFFIRMATION
I AM DIRECTLY CONNECTED TO THE SOURCE

MUDRA FOR PREVENTING STRESS

Sit with a straight back, shoulders down, nice and relaxed. Place a Crystal in your left hand, bend your elbows and bring your forearms in front of your solar plexus area parallel to the ground. Turn the palms up and rest the back of the left hand in the palm of the right hand. Both palms facing up, fingers are held together. The Crystal is positioned on the fingers of your left hand, held by thumb fingertips. The rest of the fingers are straight and together. Hold for three minutes and concentrate on your breath.

BREATH
LONG, DEEP AND SLOW THRU YOUR NOSE

AFFIRMATION
I AM IN MY OWN SAFE SPACE OF TOTAL CALM

MUDRA FOR SEXUAL BALANCE

Sit with a straight back, shoulders down, nice and relaxed. Place one medium size Crystal or two smaller Crystals in the palms of your hands. Hold your elbows slightly to the sides and clasp your hands together. The fingers are intertwined. The right thumb on top of the left thumb will empower the male side of your nature, and the left thumb on top of the right will empower the feminine, emotional side of your nature. Practice each position for a minute and half. Feel the Crystal magnify the natural polarity in your hands, and sense its stabilizing effect on your delicate creative balance. Practice for three minutes.

BREATH
LONG, DEEP AND SLOW THRU YOUR NOSE

AFFIRMATION
MY SEXUALITY IS VIBRANT AND HARMONIOUS

MUDRA FOR HELP WITH A DIET

Sit with a straight back, shoulders down, nice and relaxed. Place a small Crystal in each hand and with your hands slightly cupped, lightly fold your thumbs over the small Crystals to keep them in place. Extend your arms in front of you parallel to the ground, palms facing up, slightly cupped. Inhale and move your hands to the sides, and as you exhale, return your hands to their original position in front of you, but with your palms facing each other. Keep the palms apart and feel the life force magnifying between your hands. Repeat for Three minutes.

BREATH
LONG, DEEP INHALATION AS YOU EXPAND THE ARMS,
AND EXHALATION AS YOU RETURN THEM IN FRONT OF YOU

AFFIRMATION
I AM NOURISHED, I AM SATISFIED

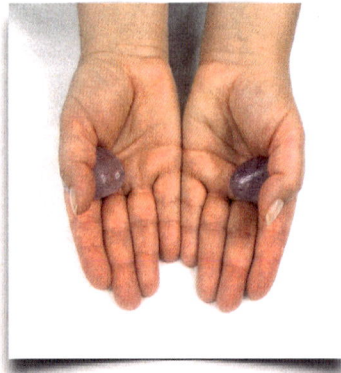

MUDRA FOR STRONG NERVES

Sit with a straight back, shoulders down, nice and relaxed. Take a small Crystal in each hand. Lift your left hand to ear level, palm facing out. Hold a small Crystal between the thumb and middle finger of the left hand, and stretch out the other fingers. Hold your right hand in front of the solar plexus, palm facing up. Hold the other small Crystal between the thumb and little finger, while the other fingers are straight. Hold for three minutes and concentrate on your breath. **This position is reversed for men.**

BREATH
Inhale in four counts and exhale in one strong breath

AFFIRMATION
I AM RESILIENT, I AM SOLID

MUDRA FOR POWERFUL ENERGY

Sit with a straight back, shoulders down, nice and relaxed. Place one or two smaller Crystals in your hands. Lift your hands in front of you at the solar plexus level. Hold your ring fingers straight, together alongside while interlacing all other fingers. The right thumb is on top of the left. Hold for three minutes and concentrate on your breath.

BREATH
LONG, DEEP AND SLOW THRU YOUR NOSE

MANTRA
OOOOONG *(God as a Creator in Manifestation)*

AFFIRMATION
I GATHER MY POWER. I GATHER MY STRENGTH

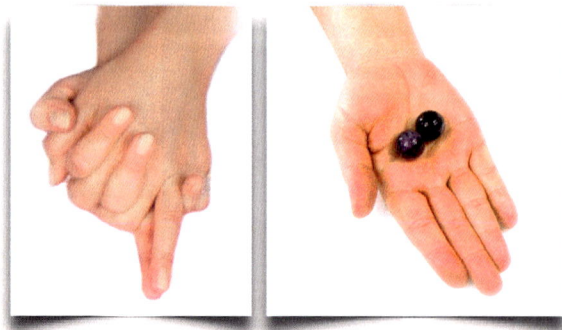

MUDRA FOR HEALTHY EYES

Sit with a straight back, shoulders down, nice and relaxed. Place a small Crystal in each hand and with your hands slightly cupped, fold your thumbs over the small Crystals to keep them in place. Bring your arms up, at your sides, the palms turned in, towards you. Now bring your palms together in front of your face, as if drawing a curtain. Open your arms, inhale, and look into the far away distance. Next, exhale while moving your hands in front of your eyes and readjust the focus while looking into your palms. Practice every two hours for three minutes, without your glasses, when you are working at a computer.

BREATH
LONG, DEEP AND SLOW THRU YOUR NOSE

MANTRA
OM *(God in his Absolute State)*

AFFIRMATION
I SOOTHE, REFRESH AND REGENERATE MY EYES

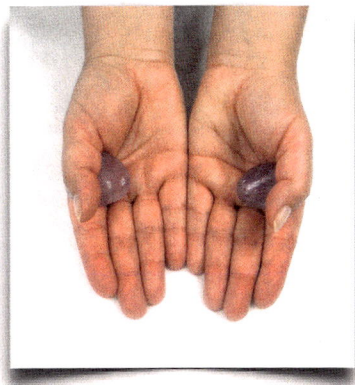

MUDRA FOR SELF ~ HEALING

    Sit with a straight back, shoulders down, nice and relaxed. Place a Crystal in the palms of your hands. You can use a larger Crystal. Bring your arms up in front of your face, fingers spread and outstretched. The Crystal is resting in the center of your palms. Connect the thumbs along their length and connect the tips of the small fingers. Inhale deeply and slowly through the nose and then close off the nostrils by placing the thumb tips over them. Hold the breath for as long as you can. Release the thumbs slightly to open the nostrils and exhale. Again hold the breath for as long as possible before inhaling. Practice for three minutes.

BREATH
AS DESCRIBED ABOVE.

AFFIRMATION
I ACTIVATE MY BODY's SELF - HEALING ABILITY

MUDRA FOR PREVENTING EXHAUSTION

Sit with a straight back, shoulders down, nice and relaxed. Place a small Crystal in the palm of each hand. Clasp the Crystals with the middle, ring and small fingers of each hand. Lift your arms and grasp your earlobes with your thumbs and index fingers. Hold on to your earlobes and let the weight of your hands gently pull on them. Relax and feel the energy shifting in your head and body. Hold for three minutes and relax.

BREATH
LONG, DEEP AND SLOW THRU YOUR NOSE
MANTRA
SAT NAM *(Truth Is God's Name, One in Spirit)*
AFFIRMATION
I CONSERVE MY ENERGY AND EVOKE MY VIGOR

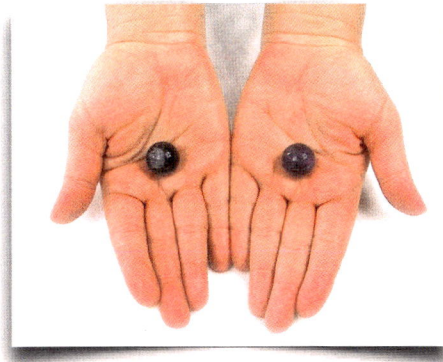

MUDRA FOR PHYSICAL STRENGTH

Sit with a straight back, shoulders down, nice and relaxed. Place a Crystal in the palms of your hands. Lift your hands up to the level of the heart and press the palms closely together. The Crystal is resting in the palms of your hands and all fingers are spread apart. The thumbs are gently touching and the index and middle fingers are barely touching. Apply maximum force to the ring and little fingers. Concentrate on the difference between finger pressure. After three minutes relax, stretch arms above your head, let down easy and rest.

BREATH
LONG, DEEP AND SLOW THRU YOUR NOSE
MANTRA
SAT NAM *(Truth Is God's Name, One in Spirit)*
AFFIRMATION
MY POWER IS CONSTANT AND LIMITLESS

MUDRA FOR REJUVENATION

Sit with a straight back, keep your shoulders down, nice and relaxed. Hold a small Crystal in the palm of each hand. Place both palms directly on your ears. Massage your ears in a circular motion away from your face, in a counter clockwise direction. Fell the gentle roll of the Crystals on your earlobes as you massage your ears. Listen to the sound of "the ocean" you create with the palms of your hands and continue for at least three minutes.

BREATH
LONG, DEEP AND SLOW THRU YOUR NOSE
MANTRA
OM *(God in His Absolute State)*
AFFIRMATION
I AM ONE WITH THE INFINITE POWER OF THE OCEAN

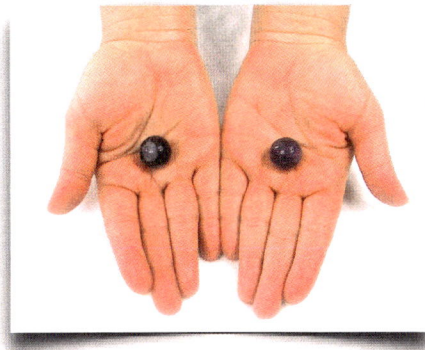

Mudra for Relaxation & Joy

Sit with a straight back, keep your shoulders down, nice and relaxed. Take a Crystal into your left hand and hold it in a fist. If you are using a Crystal wand, make sure the tip is pointing towards the sky. Lift your hands up in front of your chest. Your left hand is in a fist with the thumb tucked inside. Wrap your right hand around the left and place your right thumb over the base of the left thumb. Concentrate on your Third eye area and hold for three minutes.

BREATH
LONG, DEEP AND SLOW THRU YOUR NOSE
MANTRA
HAREE HAR HAREE HAR *(God in His Creative Aspect)*
AFFIRMATION
I AM RELAXED, CAREFREE AND JOYOUS

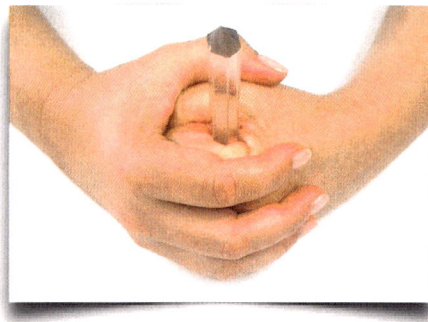

MUDRA FOR UNIVERSAL ENERGY & ETERNITY

Sit with a straight back, keep your shoulders down, nice and relaxed. Place a Crystal in center of the palm in each hand. Bend your elbows, bring your hands up and away from your body to form two V's. You can keep your arms slightly closer and lightly touching your body, to establish a stronger sense of powerful energy in your chest area, or leave some room between elbows and your body. Raise your palms to your heart level, keeping all fingers together. Feel the nurturing energy flowing into your hands. Hold for three minutes and relax.

BREATH
LONG, DEEP AND SLOW THRU YOUR NOSE

MANTRA
HAR HARE HAREE WAHE GURU
*(God, the Creator of Supreme Power and Wisdom,
the Spiritual Teacher and Guide Through Darkness)*

AFFIRMATION
THE UNIVERSE IS MY ETERNAL LIFE SOURCE

Natural Aragonite Star

Chapter Eight
Mudras & Crystals
MENTAL PROTECTION SHIELD

Mudra for Willpower of Manifestation & Amethyst Sphere

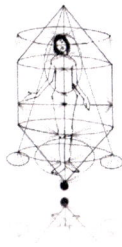

Your Mind is Your Command Center

Your mind-energy body is a mighty powerful and influential energy field, however it is very sensitive to outside stimuli and influences. We are all unique and some of us are mentally stronger than others, but we are all vulnerable and easily affected by a disruptive environment. The state of inner calm can be upset by an excessively analytical mind or negative thinking pattern. The greatest obstacle that prevents you from maintaining an unwavering mindset is fear. When you are continuously afraid of something, your biggest concerns may actually realize. The Universe receives your feared visualized image, and manifests your negative projection. In order to prevent this from occurring, you need to be in charge of your mind and avoid obsessing about worst outcomes. A strong and unwavering mindset is important for protection on numerous levels. Intentionally abolishing fear from your mind will help secure and maintain a powerful subtle energy protection shield.

Thoughts have an immense power of materialization. If used poorly, the results will be unfavorable. If used wisely and consciously, the results will be in harmony with the Divine design. You can't force an outcome, however you may visualize the best version of it. In time, you will find wisdom and a hidden blessing in a final conclusion. We don't always know what is best for our evolutionary progress, and usually recognize it much later. An overactive mind can also easily influence your heart and push you into justifying, reasoning and negotiating with your feelings. The mind has a tendency to rationalize and explain anything and everything to suit the needs of the ego. A restless and troubled mind can ruin the most wonderful moments or opportunities. It can push you into misunderstanding pure emotions and misjudging honest gestures of kindness or love.

Contrarily, a calm mind can find a brilliant solution to a seemingly unresolvable crisis. The moment your mind becomes still, a magical transformation takes place. You cease to be the limited version of yourself, but reach for the very peak of your ultimate potential. The limitations of your mind rule your daily life and influence what you attract and experience. An expanded and open mind has an instant advantage of seeing the larger picture with incredible speed, while simultaneously gaining the answers you need. Attunement with your expanded mental ability opens an invisible doorway and grants access to much of your ancient inner wisdom, that you might have forgotten. In fact, you alone possess all the answers you'll ever need. You can easily call upon your inner wisdom and intuition when your higher consciousness is working in perfect synchrony with your mind. This becomes the true alchemy you carry within. Your intuitive answer, the missing part of a puzzle, is found on command and you know precisely where it belongs. That is your mind in perfect harmony. Once you understand and master this ability, your mind will always work with you and not against you.

Mookaite Jasper

Any kind of negative personal inner dialogue or projection will weaken your mental abilities. When your overall mind frequency descends, you become open and vulnerable to negative mental suggestions, outside influences, attacks and manipulative or negative projections of others or your environment.

In a weak mental state, someone's careless and critical comment may break you, cause you self-doubt, and discourage you. Your mind requires continuous protection, so that nothing can upset your self-confidence, no doubts can make you vulnerable, and no one's negative suggestions can influence you to become endangered or self-destructive. These days, your mind is very vulnerable. With the rapid advancement of technology, it is often quite a challenge to properly differentiate real from unreal, or truth from fiction. Recognizing someone's true intentions when they are hiding behind misleading technology can be difficult. Because of increasing social media addiction, this challenge will only accelerate in the future.

Tiger's Eye

**THE MORE MANKIND DISTANCES ITSELF FROM NATURE,
THE LESS CAPABLE AND MORE DEPENDENT WE WILL BECOME.
OUR BRILLIANT MINDS WILL BE EASILY SURPASSED
BY ARTIFICIAL INTELLIGENCE, WHICH DOES NOT POSSESS A HEART.
THEREIN LIES GRAVE DANGER.**

We must strive to master our ability to discern, see beyond the obvious and accelerate our naturally given abilities. This requires practice. How resilient is your mindset against a lower frequency disruption? Your mind carries ancient knowledge that is unique to you and your soul's far-away past. It also carries old patterns that may not be to your advantage and can manifest in countless ways, such as your disposition, nature, way of thinking or receptivity.

How connected are you to inner guidance, and how receptive are you to Divine intelligence? The answer lies within your sense of spirituality and your trust in Divine Universal energy. The mind patterns that influence the undercurrent of your daily behavior and mental disposition can be altered, improved and if necessary, eliminated. It is a matter of conquering a bad habit and establishing a new, positive routine. Every habit can be undone, while recognizing and understanding oneself is the necessary first step. Oddly enough, we are usually preoccupied with observing, admiring or criticizing others while keeping ourselves out of that same scrutiny. For some individuals, seeing themselves for who they really are is harder than for others.

When you are determined about eliminating an undesirable tendency, immediately establish a new positive habit that will replace the old one. You have a certain amount of "room" for your habits and unless an undesirable one is immediately replaced with a new and healthier one, your mind will automatically slip back into the old "gear". It is like a well trained muscle. This reprograming will require some time, depending on the nature of the habit.

**YOU CAN SUCCESSFULLY ELIMINATE AN UNDESIRABLE HABIT
AND REPLACE IT WITH A DESIRABLE ONE.
WORK ON THIS FOR A FEW WEEKS
AND YOU WILL BE ABLE TO FIRMLY ANCHOR IT IN A FEW MONTHS.**

One of the most challenging undertakings for your mind is change. It requires familiarizing yourself with something new, becoming comfortable with it and adapting to a new way of functioning. Babies are most eager to explore and change, while older people are most resistant to implementing something new into their daily routine. Change requires elasticity of the brain and adaptability of the mind. It pushes you out of your comfort zone and into new experiences. The more you open to change, the more your knowledge, understanding and perception expands. You are using your senses, your mind is energized and occupied with new discoveries and challenges. This is healthy and invigorating.

Working with Mudras and Crystals is a new and most beneficial change. When you intention for clarity of mind is clear, Crystals become great power-tools and allies. For your mind's optimal functioning, establish a daily Mudra practice routine. It will strengthen your mind's resilience in times of adversity. Mudras and Crystals will accelerate your ability for acute awareness, discernment and help you evaluate challenging situations that you may face.

Each day we are bombarded with an alarmingly high amount of radio-frequency electromagnetic radiation from all the electronic devices that surround us. While we can't see them, these frequencies affect our overall health as well as cognitive abilities, more specifically our minds. If we knew all the dangerous side effects of electronics that we absorb on a daily basis, we would surely protect our energy field. Radio-frequency electromagnetic radiation depletes and interferes with healthy functioning of your natural delicate and sensitive subtle body. This may cause physical illness, and a depleted state of mental awareness. As a consequence, we become vulnerable to making poor decisions and choices while succumbing to negative thinking patterns. This can result in unhealthy destructive behavior and addictions. People suffering from addictions have an extremely sensitive subtle energy system that is easily influenced and overcome by negative frequencies. The more they succumb to addiction, the weaker their energy field becomes. Others, who are simply of delicate mind constitution will likely suffer from low self-esteem, lack of enthusiasm and willpower. These energetically vulnerable states can be overcome and remedied when your overall frequency level is maintained in a healthy high frequency range. This requires a conscious and dedicated effort. Mudras and Crystals are excellent partners on this mission.

THE CRYSTAL'S NATURAL HIGH VIBRATION WILL UPLIFT AND MAINTAIN THE HIGHEST FREQUENCY OF YOUR MIND SO THAT IT CAN FUNCTION AT YOUR OPTIMAL CAPACITY.

By helping sustain your higher frequency state, Mudras and Crystals will create a natural protective vibrational shield. Your mind will overcome and resist the unhealthy environmental radio-frequency electromagnetic radiation and maintain a healthy function. When creating a mental frequency shield, select Crystals that are very specific for clearing electromagnetic field. Clearly imprint your intention when programing your Crystal, so that it will work for this specific purpose. With Mudra and Crystal practice presented in this chapter, the intention and focus is on establishing, strengthening and preserving the balance and harmony of your mental body.

MUDRA FOR MENTAL BALANCE

Sit with a straight back, shoulders down, nice and relaxed. Place a Crystal in the center of the palm in each open hand. Bend your elbows, lift the hands up in front of your solar plexus or chest area and interlace the fingers backward with palms facing up. Fingers are pointing up and are straight. Practice for Three minutes.

BREATH
LONG, DEEP AND SLOW THRU YOUR NOSE
MANTRA
GOBINDAY, MUKUNDAY, UDARAAY, APAARAY,
HARYING, KARYNG, NIRNAMAY, AKAMAY
(Sustainer, Liberator, Enlightener, Infinite, Destroyer, Creator, Nameless, Desire-less)
AFFIRMATION
MY MIND IS IN PERFECT BALANCE AND HARMONY

MUDRA FOR FACING FEAR

Sit with a straight back, shoulders down, nice and relaxed. Place a Crystal into the center of your left palm, while keeping it open. Hold the left hand in front of your navel, palm facing up, fingers together. Bend your right elbow and lift the arm up to level of your face. Face your right palm outward, as if taking a vow. Fingers are together. Concentrate on energy flowing into your hands, magnified by the Crystal. Practice for Three minutes.

BREATH
LONG, DEEP AND SLOW THRU YOUR NOSE
MANTRA
NIRBHAO NIRVAIR AKAAL MORT
(Fearless, Without Enemy, Immortal Personified God)
AFFIRMATION
I AM FEARLESS , I AM BRAVE

MUDRA FOR TAKING AWAY HARDSHIPS

Sit with a straight back, shoulders down, nice and relaxed. Place a Crystal into each hand and close them into fists, while keeping the thumbs on the outside. Now swing your arms in big circles, like a pendulum. Begin with the movement holding hands outstretched to the side. Next, bend your elbows and swing fists up and forward towards you, as you inhale, then again opening your arms, stretching elbows and returning back to original position as you exhale. Repeat for Three minutes and relax.

BREATH
LONG, DEEP AND SLOW THRU YOUR NOSE
MANTRA
HAR HARE GOBINDAY, HAR HARE MUKUNDAY
(He Is My Sustainer, He Is My Liberator)
AFFIRMATION
MY PATH FORWARD IS OPEN AND CLEAR

MUDRA FOR CALMING YOUR MIND

Sit with a straight back, shoulders down, nice and relaxed. Take a small Crystal into your right hand. Cross your arms in front of your chest, elbows bent at a ninety-degree angle. Arms are parallel to the ground. Place your Crystal on the exterior of your left lower-arm, near the elbow, and cover it with your right hand. Let the Crystal rest in the center of your right palm. The right hand is on top of the left arm and left hand below the right arm. All fingers are together and straight. Keep your elbows from sinking. Hold for Three minutes, then relax and be still.

BREATH
LONG, DEEP AND SLOW THRU YOUR NOSE
MANTRA
OM (*God in his absolute state*)
AFFIRMATION
I AM SERENE AND COMPOSED

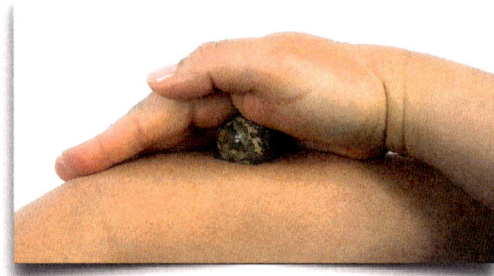

MUDRA FOR DIMINISHING WORRIES

Sit with a straight back, shoulders down, nice and relaxed. Place a medium or large Crystal in your hands. Bring the hands up in front of your heart with palms facing up. The sides of the little fingers and the inner sides of the palms are touching. Now bring your middle fingers tips together, and extend the thumbs away from the palms. The Crystal is resting in the center of your palms. Keep the fingers stretched as little antennas for energy. Hold for Three minutes, then relax and be still.

BREATH
LONG, DEEP AND SLOW THRU YOUR NOSE

AFFIRMATION
I RELEASE ALL WORRY AND FEEL ASSURED

Mudra for Self ~ Identification

Sit with a straight back, shoulders down, nice and relaxed. Place a small Crystal sphere in each hand, and hold it between the middle part of the thumb and index fingers. If your Crystal is smaller or is a thumb stone, hold it between the thumb and index fingertips. The rest of the fingers are together and stretched out. Both hands are held in this position. The left arm is at your waist, touching your body, elbow bent at a ninety degree angle with palm looking up towards the sky. The right arm is bent, touching your body, hand brought up to shoulder level, palm is facing down. Hold for Three minutes, then relax and be still.

BREATH
LONG, DEEP AND SLOW THRU YOUR NOSE

AFFIRMATION
I PERCEIVE, RESPECT AND UNDERSTAND WHO I AM

MUDRA FOR CONCENTRATION

    Sit with a straight back, shoulders down, nice and relaxed. Bend your elbows and bring your arms to your chest. Place a small Crystal in each hand, each thumb and index finger should form a circle so that the index finger is curled far into the beginning of the thumb. Place the Crystal in the small circle area. The other fingers are connected, stretched and pointing up. Place your hands and outstretched fingers back to back. Be still, concentrate on your Third Eye. Hold for Three minutes, then relax.

BREATH
LONG, DEEP AND SLOW THRU YOUR NOSE

MANTRA
AKAL AKAL AKAL HARI AKAL *(Immortal Creator)*

AFFIRMATION
MY MIND IS CENTERED, FOCUSED AND CLEAR

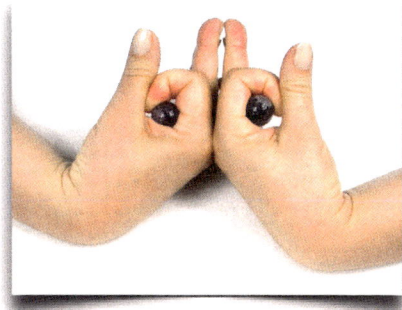

MUDRA FOR INNER SECURITY

Sit with a straight back, shoulders down, nice and relaxed. Place a small Crystal in each hand and with your hands lightly cupped, fold your thumbs over the small Crystals to keep them in place. Begin by placing your hands in reversed prayer pose: hands touching back to back at the level of your heart. Hold the pose for a beat, then turn them over and hold with palms pressed together in the prayer Mudra of Divine Worship. Hold for a beat and repeat. Practice for Three minutes, then relax.

BREATH
LONG, DEEP AND SLOW THRU YOUR NOSE
MANTRA
AD SHAKTI AD SHAKTI
(I Bow to the Creator's Power)
AFFIRMATION
I AM SAFE AND SECURE, I AM SHELTERED AND PROTECTED

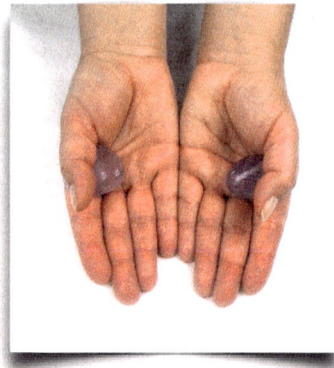

MUDRA FOR SELF ~ CONFIDENCE

Sit with a straight back, shoulders down, nice and relaxed. Place a small Crystal in each hand. Lift your hands up to the level of your solar plexus with elbows bent to the sides. Hold each Crystal with the bent middle, ring, and little fingers of each hand. Align the middle, ring and little fingers of both hands back to back. Extend and press the index fingertips together and extend and press the thumb tips together. The thumbs are pointed towards you and the index fingers away from you. Hold for Three minutes, then relax.

BREATH
LONG, DEEP AND SLOW THRU YOUR NOSE

MANTRA
EK ONG KAR SAT GURU PRASAD, SAT GURU PRASAD EK ONG KAR
(The Creator Is the One That Dispels Darkness and Illuminates Us by His Grace)

AFFIRMATION
I AM READY, WILLING AND ABLE TO ACCOMPLISH MY GOALS

MUDRA FOR EMPOWERING YOUR VOICE

Sit with a straight back, shoulders down, nice and relaxed. Place a medium size Crystal in your hands. Bend your elbows and hold them parallel to the ground as you bring your hands up in front of you at the level of your throat. Turn the right palm outward and the left palm toward you. Now bend your fingers and hook your hands together, the left hand on the outside. The Crystal is resting between both hands. Gently pull on the hands as if trying to pull them apart, while keeping your shoulders down. The Crystal sits at the place of most tension. Hold for Three minutes, then relax.

BREATH
LONG, DEEP AND SLOW THRU YOUR NOSE

AFFIRMATION
MY WORDS INSPIRE, MOTIVATE AND CELEBRATE

MUDRA FOR PATIENCE

Sit with a straight back, shoulders down, nice and relaxed. Place a small Crystal or a worry-thumb-stone in each hand. Connect the fingertips of the thumbs and middle fingers, and hold the Crystals between the fingertips. The rest of the fingers are outstretched. Lift your arms up at your sides so that your hands are at the level of your ears, palms facing outward. Hold for Three minutes, then relax.

BREATH
LONG, DEEP AND SLOW THRU YOUR NOSE
MANTRA
EK ONG KAR SAT GURU PRASAAD
(One Creator, Illuminated by God's Grace)
AFFIRMATION
I AM PATIENT, COMPOSED AND POISED

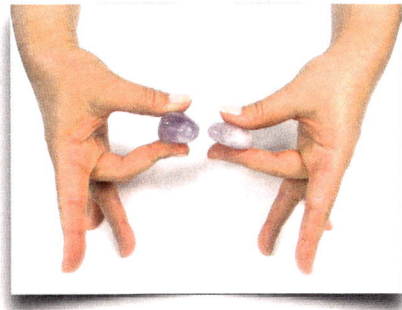

MUDRA FOR PROSPERITY

Sit with a straight back, shoulders down, nice and relaxed. Place a small Crystal in each hand and with your hands cupped, lightly fold your thumbs over the small Crystals to keep them in place. Bring your hands in front of you, the rest of the fingers are held together and palms are facing down. Press the alongside the index fingers together and hold for a moment. Now turn your hands over so that the palms are facing up towards the sky for a moment and the sides of the little fingers are touching. Keep repeating and chant the mantra HAR with each change of hand position. Continue the practice for Eleven minutes and rest.

BREATH
SHORT, FAST BREATH OF FIRE FROM THE POINT OF THE NAVEL,
REPEAT WITH EACH MANTRA AND MUDRA MOVEMENT

MANTRA
HAR HAR *(God, God)*

AFFIRMATION
I ATTRACT PROSPERITY, ABUNDANCE AND GOOD FORTUNE

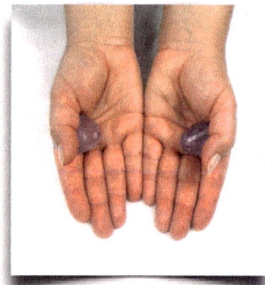

MUDRA FOR EFFICIENCY

Sit with a straight back, shoulders down, nice and relaxed. Take a small Crystal into your hands. Bring your arms up in front of your heart, the palms turned in, toward you. The palm of the right hand is placed outside on top of the left hand. All fingers are straight. Hold the Crystal between your thumb tips and keep them firmly pressed together. The forearms are parallel to the ground. Hold for Three minutes, then relax.

BREATH
INHALE SLOWLY AND DEEPLY, HOLD FOR TEN SECONDS,
AND EXHALE FOR TEN SECONDS

MANTRA
ATMA PARMATMA GURU HARI
(Soul, Supreme Soul, the Teacher in His Supreme Power and Wisdom)

AFFIRMATION
I AM EFFICIENT, ADEPT AND EFFECTIVE

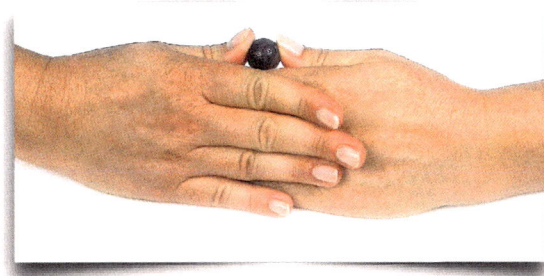

MUDRA FOR TRANQUILIZING YOUR MIND

Sit with a straight back, shoulders down, nice and relaxed. Place two similarly sized Crystals in your hands. Bend your elbows and bring your hands up to your chest. Connect the middle fingertips and stretch them outward. Hold the Crystals with the bent index, ring and little fingers of both hands, and press them together along the second or third joint, depending on the size of the Crystal. Connect your thumb tips and extend them toward you. Hold for Three minutes, then relax.

BREATH
LONG, DEEP AND SLOW THRU YOUR NOSE
MANTRA
MAN HAR TAN HAR GURU HAR
(Mind with God, Soul with God, the Divine Guide and His Supreme Wisdom)
AFFIRMATION
I AM SERENE, PEACEFUL AND TRANQUIL

MUDRA FOR WISDOM

Sit with a straight back and keep your shoulders down, nice and relaxed. Take two smaller Crystals into your hands. Bend your elbows and lift them up to the side, parallel to the ground. Make gentle fists, leaving the index fingers out. Hold a Crystal in each fist. Now hook your outstretched index fingers around each other. The right palm is facing down and the left toward your chest. Gently pull on the index fingers throughout the practice. Hold for Three minutes, then relax.

BREATH
LONG, DEEP AND SLOW THRU YOUR NOSE
MANTRA
SAT NAM *(Truth Is God's Name, One in Spirit)*
AFFIRMATION
MY INNER WISDOM IS ANCIENT AND INFINITE

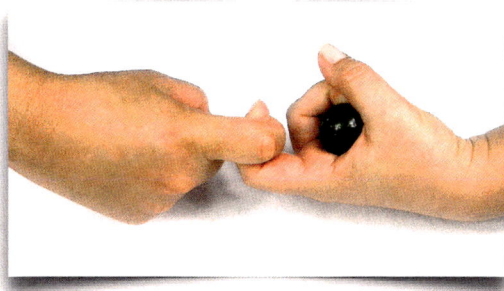

MUDRA FOR POWER OF PROJECTION

Sit with a straight back and keep your shoulders down, nice and relaxed. Take two Crystal wands into your hands. Bring your hands up to the level between your solar plexus and the heart region. Hold a Crystal wand in each hand, tucked in the palm and clasped with bent third and ring fingers, and press them together back to back from second to third knuckle. Interlace both index fingers and both small fingers. Press the thumbs against the upper side of the right index finger. The Crystal wands are pointing towards the sky. Practice for Eleven minutes, then relax.

BREATH
SHORT BREATH OF FIRE WITH CONTINUOUS RHYTHM OF THE MANTRA

MANTRA
HAR HAR HAR (*God, God, God*)

AFFIRMATION
I ALIGN MY FREQUENCY WITH MY HIGHER PURPOSE

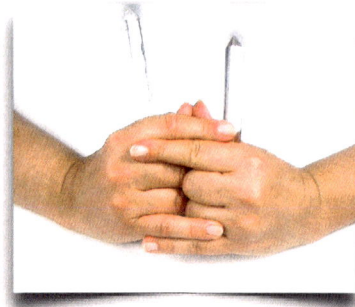
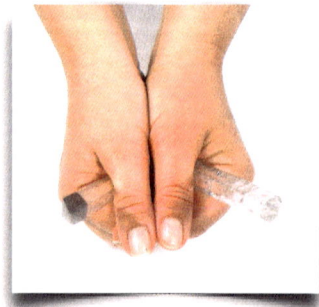

MUDRA FOR LOOKING INTO THE FUTURE

Sit with a straight back and keep your shoulders down, nice and relaxed. Place a smaller Crystal in each hand and with your hands slightly cupped, fold your thumbs over the small Crystals to keep them in place. Bring your hands up to the level of your face and keep them in front and to the sides of your head. Palms are facing each other. This Mudra is different from *Mudra for Clarity of Decision*. Here palms are turned towards each other and on the sides of your face. Practice for Three minutes, then relax.

BREATH
LONG, DEEP AND SLOW THRU YOUR NOSE

MANTRA
OMM (*God in His Absolute State*)

AFFIRMATION
I CLEARLY SENSE THE OPTIMAL POTENTIAL OF MY FUTURE

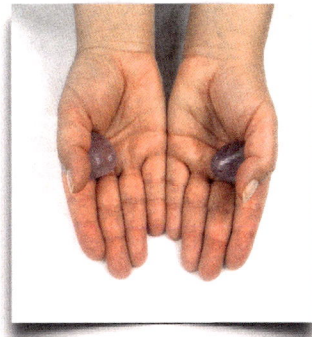

Mudra for Willpower of Manifestation

Sit with a straight back and shoulders down, nice and relaxed. Place a Crystal between your hand's wrists and hold it in place with slight pressure of wrists against each other. Extend both arms and lift them in front of you at your heart level, parallel to the ground. While holding the wrists together, flex the palms, as though pushing against a wall. All the fingers remain stretched and spread out. Thumbs are pointing upwards. Keep the shoulders down, fully stretch the elbows and maintain this position for Eleven minutes, then relax.

BREATH
LONG, DEEP AND SLOW THRU YOUR NOSE

MANTRA
SATNAM, SATNAM, SATNAM,
SATNAM, SATNAM, SATNAM, WAHE GURU
(Truth is God's Name, one in Spirit, His is the Supreme Wisdom)

AFFIRMATION
I MANIFEST MY DREAMS, I MATERIALIZE MY VISION

MUDRA FOR VICTORY

Sit with a straight back and keep your shoulders down, nice and relaxed. Take a medium size Crystal in each hand. Make gentle fists with both hands while holding the Crystals. Lift up your arms and cross them in over your upper chest, left over right. This powerful Mudra is seen in many sculptures of Egyptian Pharaohs. Practice for Three minutes, then relax.

BREATH
LONG, DEEP AND SLOW THRU YOUR NOSE

MANTRA
OMM *(God in His Absolute State)*

AFFIRMATION
I AM VICTORIOUS AND SUCCESSFUL

Ocean Jasper Palm Stone

Chapter Nine

Mudras & Crystals

EMOTIONAL PROTECTION SHIELD

Mudra for Healing a Broken Heart & Amethyst Sphere

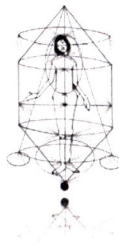

YOUR HEART IS THE SEAT OF YOUR SOUL

Securing and building a protective shield for your emotional energy body is possibly the greatest challenge. Why? Because a heart does not obey a request or command. It has certain old energy attachments and memories that navigate your deeper longings and desires. Your capacity for love, forgiveness, compassion, acceptance and generosity is determined by your deep emotional patterns. Furthermore, your ability to emit and receive unconditional love affects the entire state of your well-being. In short, how you love is how you live.

This layer of your energy body is most delicate, highly sensitive, and fluctuates with every tiny disturbance. It is interconnected with your physical and mental energy body and if you are in physical pain or mental anguish, emotions will ripple in waves that can turn you over like a tiny boat in the ocean. But it works the other way around as well, your irritate emotions will disrupt your mind and certainly affect your physical body. If you suffer from an emotional upset, you will become mentally impaired which could cause a physical injury or general sense of unwell. We each have a vulnerable area, whether it is physical, mental, emotional or spiritual. It is important to strive for an overall balance of these three aspects, so you can easily manage life's challenges and avoid overwhelm.

The delicate layer of your emotional subtle body endures much from outside influences. The depleted and unharmonious lower frequency energy states stem from imbalance of the first three chakras which are vulnerable to emotions based in fear. This can be overcome by consciously cultivating love in your heart. To establish a vibrant and healthy emotional energy state, work thru your feelings, acknowledge them, and express them. Eventually you will successfully transform and ascend your emotional energy state to a healing and loving disposition towards yourself and others.

Everything in life is in constant motion, unexpected events may occur every day that can upset the balance between your body, mind and heart. Adaptability to change can be gained with time in peaceful reflection. Listen, recognize, respect and express your emotions, for they are as important as exercise for your body and inner reflection for your mind. Emotions reveal your hidden true nature and offer access to your intuitive compass of self-realization.

If your emotional subtle body is affected by unharmonious mental states such as insecurity or anxiety, your heart will suffer consequences. Emotional pain, sorrow or grief, will restrict your ability to open up, recognize true love or welcome new love into your life. If you are holding onto unfulfilled or unresolved relationships from your past, these energy cords will keep you "hostage". Such challenging energy blockages will prevent you from regaining your emotional freedom and moving into new and happier experiences. Unresolved emotional injuries can energetically and physically weaken you and make you susceptible to unhealthy energy attachments. When another person is tied to your emotional wound, it will require a considerable effort to heal the open access to your energy body and form a subtle protective shield. Therefore it is necessary to understand your vulnerabilities and consciously close an energy tear in your Aura.

Rutilated Quartz

Finding peace with conflicting emotional dynamics of your past is necessary and will likely keep changing, transforming, and evolving until it eventually resolves. Acknowledge your fears and old grief, for that is the only way to eliminate and heal them. Of course, we may not always be able to find perfect closure thru an in-person exchange or communication, however, you can establish an anchor of peace on the subtle energy realm. If you imprint resolution and closure within your own emotional field, the other person's access to your subtle energy field is interrupted and broken off. The free access to you is therefore prevented and terminated.

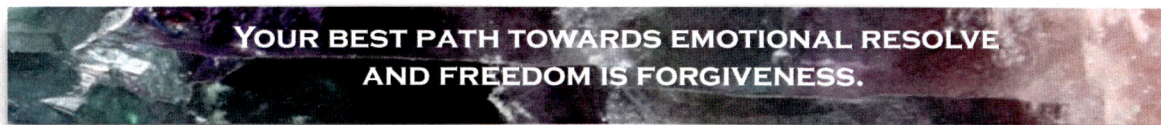

YOUR BEST PATH TOWARDS EMOTIONAL RESOLVE AND FREEDOM IS FORGIVENESS.

Our lives would be much easier if we began each day with an emotionally balanced state. Imagine how every mishap would not send you into a frenzy, how other people's reckless words would not affect you, and how you'd tackle daily problems from a state of objective observation, instead of reactive fear and anxiety. Your effort for conscious transformation is one of the most important missions of your life.

We bring into this life many unresolved emotional states. Love never dies and unrequited love will follow you through lifetimes, until it is fulfilled or transformed and restructured in such a way, that is can find a proper harmonious expression. Love is our driving force. Even the most desperate need for attention and validation has its roots in basic need for love. If a person does not receive essential nurturing and love in their childhood, they will spend their entire life chasing after it or suffering from permanent depletion and extreme neediness. Love is the most basic requirement of our human life.

By keeping your emotional balance throughout the day, your physical health will much improve and your mental state will be less burdened by obsessive thinking patterns and over - analyzing of hurtful occurrences from your past. Your disposition will be calm and centered, and you will become quite untouchable to external forces. You will attracts similarly disposed individuals, and together establish a field of utmost harmony and inner calm. This is the only healthy way to live and thrive. But in order to accomplish this, you may have to eliminate certain habits and distance yourself from people and situations that perpetuate negativity.

If you always play the rescuer this will not necessarily bring you great inner calm. If you wait for someone else to rescue you, the message is clear - you feel incapable of rescuing yourself. Remember this - the way people treat you is a reflection of how you treat yourself. If you are unkind and too demanding of yourself, others with behave alike. If your inner monologue is permeated with negativity, so will words of others. If you do not have a loving relationship with yourself, others will follow your example. Self-reliance, self-realization, self-accountability are qualities to develop and strive for. Your ability to receive love and your clear intention to give love will attract loving and compatible partners and friends into your life. The Universe will reward you by bringing you kindred spirits.

Orange Calcite

Another very important aspect to be aware of is the intimate connection between your breath and emotions. Observe how you breathe when you are experiencing various emotional states. When frightened, you may hold your breath, when relieved you will utter a long exhale. When excited, your breath will be shorter and faster. What does this tell you?

YOUR EMOTIONS CONTROL YOUR BREATH AND YOUR BREATH CONTROLS YOUR EMOTIONS.

If you are experiencing an upsetting emotion and your breathing is either too fast, shallow or in a holding pattern, consciously focus on implementing long, deep and slow breath through your nose. The positive effects and change will be immediate and very effective. This will help you manage pain, anxiety, overexcitement, anger and fear. Every emotion can be brought into a state of balance with the technique of slow, deep breath through your nose. This is the main breathing technique for our Mudra practice. As I mentioned before, your breath has to be centered at the solar plexus stomach area while expanding your ribcage for inhalation and contracting for exhalation. Your shoulders should not move. This kind of breath will immediately balance your Third chakra centre - the seat of fear and anger. It will help dissipate unhealthy subtle energy congestion in Third chakra and facilitate a healthy and energizing energy flow upwards on your Chakra scale.

YOUR HEART IS THE SEAT OF YOUR SOUL IT CARRIES THE ULTIMATE POWER OF THE UNIVERSE ~ UNCONDITIONAL LOVE.

When you master absolute stillness of your body, mind and heart, you are ready for a blessing, for a revelation, for a Divine gift. It may be only momentary, but feels like an eternity, it may feel like a thousand soothing waves of the ocean, or a sense of flying thru the stars…whatever it is, it will occur with an immeasurable amount of love and care. This is the desirable outcome of your Mudra and Crystal immersion - an exalted state of all encompassing Divine love. It is not something one can imagine, or pretend to feel. It can and will only happen with truest and purest of intentions. The Universe perceives the very fibers of your desires and knows you better than you know yourself. If you strive for the ultimate inner peace and awareness, it shall be granted only when your heart is open and pure. Ascending to this level is your ultimate destination.

The practice of Mudras and Crystals is ideal for harmonizing and magnifying the frequency of your emotional energy body. Once you bring awareness to your old patterns and have a clear intention to heal your emotional wounds, you will reach a state of inner balance. You are no longer easily accessible to outside energy attachments. Your strong energy shield of protection will surround your entire being. Visualize yourself enveloped by immensely brilliant white light, glowing, impenetrable, and supremely protected by permanent infusion of Divine power. With the Mudras presented in this chapter, the intention and focus is on establishing, strengthening and preserving the balance and harmony of your emotional body.

MUDRA FOR ASCENSION OF YOUR HEART

Sit with a straight back and keep your shoulders down, nice and relaxed. Take a medium size Crystal or a set of Crystal wands in each hand. Lift your hands up and hold them in front of your chest, palms facing your heart. If you've selected Crystal wands, make sure the tips are pointing upwards, towards the sky. The Crystals are held in place with your thumbs. Let the tips of middle fingers touch, all the fingers are straight. Practice for Three minutes, then relax.

BREATH
LONG, DEEP AND SLOW THRU YOUR NOSE
MANTRA
OMM *(God in His Absolute State)*
AFFIRMATION
LOVE IS MY GUIDE, I LIVE FROM MY HEART

MUDRA FOR LOVE

Sit with a straight back and keep your shoulders down, nice and relaxed. Place two smaller Crystals in your hands and curl the middle and ring fingers into your palms and over the Crystals. Extend your index and little fingers and cross over the bent fingers with your thumbs. Raise your arms up to the level of your head. Keep your elbows from sinking. Hold for Three minutes, then relax.

BREATH
INHALE EIGHT SHORT COUNTS, WITH ONE STRONG, LONG EXHALE

MANTRA
SAT NAM WAHE GURU

(God Is Truth, His Is the Supreme Power and Wisdom)

AFFIRMATION
I BEAM LOVE AND AM ENVELOPED IN LIGHT

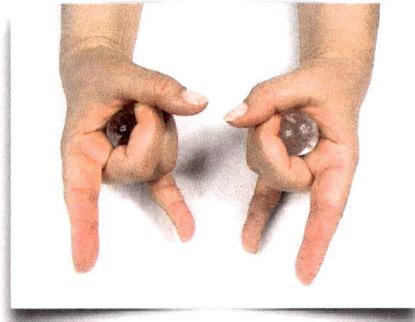

MUDRA FOR OVERCOMING ANXIETY

Sit with a straight back and keep your shoulders down, nice and relaxed. Place a medium or large size Crystal in each hand. Bend your elbows and raise your arms so your upper arms are parallel to the ground and extended out to the sides. Your hands are at the level of your ears, fingers spread wide and pointing up to the sky. Hold the Crystals in place with your thumbs, while keeping all fingers straight and apart. Start rotating your hands back and forth, pivoting at the wrists. You will go thru a period that seems difficult, but remain persistent and it will become easier. Practice for Three minutes, then relax, and enjoy the sensations.

BREATH
LONG, DEEP AND SLOW THRU YOUR NOSE

MANTRA
HARKANAM SAT NAM
(God's Name Is Truth)

AFFIRMATION
I RELEASE ALL ANXIETY AND REPLACE IT WITH PEACE

MUDRA FOR EMOTIONAL BALANCE

Before this practice, drink a glass of water to balance your system. Sit with a straight back and keep your shoulders down, nice and relaxed. Take a Crystal in each hand and wrap your hands around your body as if giving yourself a hug. Keep your palms open and gently press the Crystals against your body. Close your eyes, take a deep inhale, give yourself a strong hug and lift your shoulders towards your ears for a few moments. Hold your breath, then exhale while lowering your shoulders and loosening the embrace. Continue for Three minutes, then relax.

BREATH
LONG, DEEP AND SLOW THRU YOUR NOSE
MANTRA
SAT NAM *(Truth is God's Name)*
AFFIRMATION
I AM IN PERFECT BALANCE, MY HEART IS PEACEFUL

MUDRA FOR HELP IN A GRAVE SITUATION

Sit with a straight back and keep your shoulders down, nice and relaxed. Place a Crystal in each hand. Bend your elbows and place both palms on your upper chest, fingers together and pointing toward each other. Hold the Crystals in the center of your palms while gently pressing against your chest. Feel the healing energy of your hands soothing your heart. Hold for Three minutes, then relax.

BREATH
LONG, DEEP AND SLOW THRU YOUR NOSE
MANTRA
HUMME HUM, BRAHAM HUM, BRAHAM HUM
(Calling upon Your Infinite Self)
AFFIRMATION
I SOOTHE MY BODY, MIND, HEART AND SOUL

MUDRA FOR RELEASING NEGATIVE EMOTIONS

Sit with a straight back and keep your shoulders down, nice and relaxed. Place a Crystal in each hand, any size will work fine. Make fists with both hands, bend your arms and bring them up in front of your heart. Cross your left arm over right while keeping your fists turned outwards. Hold for Three minutes then relax.

BREATH
LONG, DEEP AND SLOW THRU YOUR NOSE
MANTRA
OMM *(God in His Absolute State)*
AFFIRMATION
I RELEASE AND LET GO
I AM FREE AND CLEAR
I AM LIGHT

Mudra for Healing a Broken Heart

Sit with a straight back and keep your shoulders down, nice and relaxed. Place a Crystal in your hands and lift them up in front of your face. Gently hold the hands together, with the tips of the middle fingers pointing towards the Third Eye area. Your hands are touching your face, the thumbs are placed around your nose and mouth. Leave some space between the little fingers and breathe through this opening. Hold for Three minutes then relax.

BREATH
Long, deep and slow as if drinking water thru the space between palms and the opening between little fingers

MANTRA
HUMME HUM HUM BRAHAM
(Calling Upon Your Infinite Self))

AFFIRMATION
MY BREATH CAN HEAL AND SOOTHE MY HEART

MUDRA FOR UPLIFTING YOUR HEART

Sit with a straight back, shoulders down, nice and relaxed. Place a small Crystal in each hand and gently fold your thumbs over them to keep them in place. The rest of your fingers are straight and together. Lift you hands and hold them above your heart, palms facing down. Your upper arms are parallel to the ground. Keep the elbows in place through the practice. The middle fingertips are touching. As you inhale, the distance between middle fingertips gets bigger; as you exhale, the middle fingertips should connect. With each inhalation feel the healing energy expand in your heart and chest area. Repeat for Three minutes, then relax.

BREATH
LONG, DEEP AND SLOW THRU YOUR NOSE

AFFIRMATION
MY HEART IS UPLIFTED AND FILLED WITH LOVE

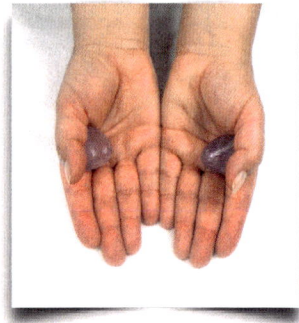

MUDRA FOR INNER INTEGRITY

Sit with a straight back and keep your shoulders down, nice and relaxed. Place a smaller size Crystal in the palm of each hand and curl your fingers over them, leaving the thumbs out. Bend your elbows and lift your upper arms so they are parallel to the ground. Bring your hands to ear level, palms facing out and point the outstretched thumbs toward your ears. Hold for Three minutes and relax.

BREATH
SHORT, FAST BREATH OF FIRE FROM NAVEL
MANTRA
SAT NAM *(Truth Is God's Name, One in Spirit)*
AFFIRMATION
I AM HONEST AND TRUE TO MYSELF
I UPHOLD MY INTEGRITY

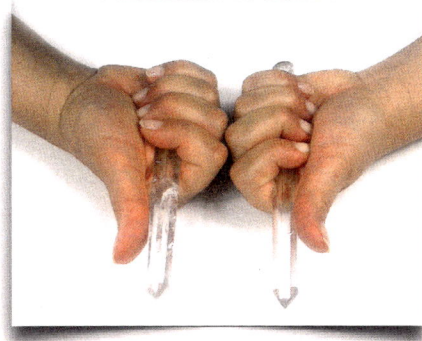

MUDRA FOR HAPPINESS

Sit with a straight back and keep your shoulders down, nice and relaxed. Place a smaller size Crystal in the palm of each hand and bend the ring and little fingers over them. Press them into the palms firmly cross over with your thumbs. Stretch the index and middle fingers and keep them together. Bend your elbows and bring your arms to your sides, away from your body. Elbows are just below the level of the shoulders. Palms are facing forward, index and middle fingers are pointing towards the sky. Hold for Three minutes and relax.

BREATH
LONG, DEEP AND SLOW THRU YOUR NOSE
MANTRA
SAT NAM *(Truth Is God's Name, one in Spirit)*
AFFIRMATION
I AM HAPPY, I AM GRATEFUL, I AM BLESSED

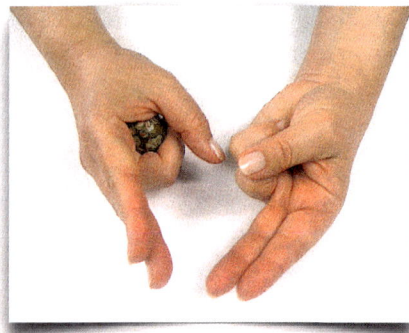

MUDRA FOR BALANCED SPEECH

Sit with a straight back and keep your shoulders down, nice and relaxed. Place a Crystal Wand in your hands and hold it with the thumb and index fingertips, while the rest of the fingers are outstretched, held apart, only fingertips touching. Lift your hands and hold them in front of your heart and throat area. Thumbs are pointing towards you, little fingers away from you and the rest of the fingers towards the sky. Elbows are out to the sides and away from your body. Hold for Three minutes and relax.

BREATH
LONG, DEEP AND SLOW THRU YOUR NOSE
MANTRA
OMM *(God in His Absolute State)*
AFFIRMATION
MY WORDS ARE IN PERFECT BALANCE,
HARMONIOUS AND CALM

MUDRA FOR NURTURING YOUR HEART

    Sit with a straight back and keep your shoulders down, nice and relaxed. Place a medium size Crystal in each hand and hold it nestled in the space between the thumb and index fingers, while they wrap around. If your Crystals are small, you can hold them between thumb and index fingertips. The rest of the fingers are outstretched and held together. Lift your hands and place them over your heart area, crossing the left hand over the right. Hold for Three minutes and relax.

BREATH
LONG, DEEP AND SLOW THRU YOUR NOSE
MANTRA
OMM *(God in His Absolute State)*
AFFIRMATION
MY HEART IS OVERFLOWING WITH LOVE

MUDRA FOR SELF - REFLECTION

Sit with a straight back and keep your shoulders down, nice and relaxed. Place a Crystal in your the palm of your left hand and close it into a fist. Wrap the right hand over the fist of the left hand. The right thumb is crossed over the left. Lift your hands and place them in front of your throat area, gently tucked under your chin. Hold for Three minutes and relax.

BREATH
LONG, DEEP AND SLOW THRU YOUR NOSE
MANTRA
SAT NAM *(Truth Is God's Name, one in Spirit)*
AFFIRMATION
I STUDY AND LEARN ABOUT MYSELF,
MY ACTIONS AND INTENTIONS

MUDRA FOR CONTENTMENT OF YOUR HEART

    Sit with a straight back and keep your shoulders down, nice and relaxed. Work with two smaller size Crystals and place one between the thumb and the middle fingertip of the right hand and the other between the thumb and the little fingertip of the left hand. Relax and gently stretch out the rest of the fingers. Hold your hands in front of your heart, a few inches apart, with both palms looking up. Practice for three minutes, then make fists with both hands and relax. **Men should practice the same position with opposite hands.**

BREATH
LONG, DEEP AND SLOW THRU YOUR NOSE
MANTRA
SARE SA SA SARE SA SA SARE HARE HAR
(God is Infinite in His Creativity)
AFFIRMATION
I NURTURE PEACE AND CONTENTMENT OF MY HEART

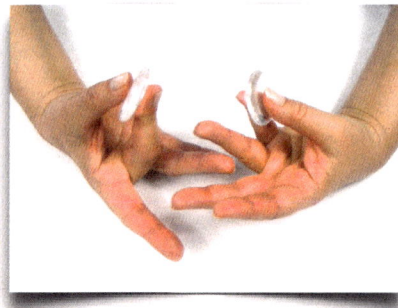

Mudra for Opening Your Heart Center

Sit with a straight back and keep your shoulders down, nice and relaxed. Work with a medium size Crystal and hold it between both hands. Lift your hands up in front of your heart and create a cup, palms facing each other, all fingers spread out and pointing up. Only the upper parts of your thumbs and pinkies and the bases of your palms are touching. Keep all fingers outstretched. Hold for Three minutes and relax.

BREATH
LONG, DEEP AND SLOW THRU YOUR NOSE
MANTRA
SAT NAM
(Truth Is God's Name, One in Spirit)
AFFIRMATION
I AM READY TO OPEN MY HEART

MUDRA OF OPEN HEART

Sit with a straight back and keep your shoulders down, nice and relaxed. Take two medium sized Crystals and place them in the center of the palm of each hand. Bend your elbows and lift your hands up in front of your upper chest. The palms are looking up toward the sky and all fingers are stretched and spread apart. The Crystals are resting in your palms. The hands are not touching. Keep the fingers stretched out as antennas of energy. Visualize your open heart filled with glowing healing rose light. Hold for Three minutes and relax.

BREATH
LONG, DEEP AND SLOW THRU YOUR NOSE
MANTRA
SAT NAM
(Truth Is God's Name, One in Spirit)
AFFIRMATION
MY HEART IS OPEN, RECEPTIVE AND WELCOMING

Mudra for Illuminating Your Heart

Sit with a straight back and keep your shoulders down, nice and relaxed. Take a Crystal into your right hand. Cross the hands in front of your heart, right hand over left. Both palms are turned towards your chest. The thumb fingers are straight and hooked together, all fingers are straight, right small finger is held apart. The Crystal is resting under the palm center of the right hand on top of the left hand. Hold for Three minutes and relax.

BREATH
Long, deep and slow thru your nose
MANTRA
OMM *(God in His Absolute State)*
AFFIRMATION
I AM A BEACON OF LIGHT

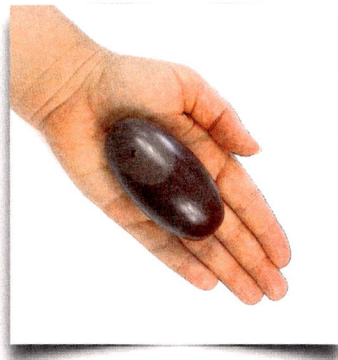

MUDRA OF TWO HEARTS

    Sit with a straight back and keep your shoulders down, nice and relaxed. Place a small Crystal between the thumb and index fingertips of each hand, while forming a circle. Extend all other fingers and keep them spread out. Lift your arms up in front of your heart, left over right, palms facing outward. Cross your wrists over each other, left arm is on the outside, and the right hand is closest to your chest. Hook your pinkies together while keeping the rest of the fingers extended. Hold for Three minutes and relax.

BREATH
LONG, DEEP AND SLOW THRU YOUR NOSE
MANTRA
SAT NAM *(Truth Is God's Name, One in Spirit)*
AFFIRMATION
I SHARE THE PERFECT HARMONY OF MY HEART

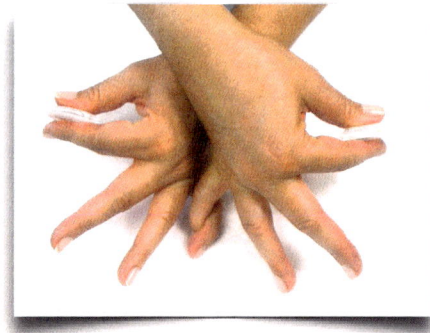

Mudra for Balancing Yin & Yang

Sit with a straight back and keep shoulders down, nice and relaxed. Place a medium size Crystal in each hand and hold it nestled in the small space between the thumb and index fingers, while they wrap around. Extend the rest of the fingers and space them apart. Lift your right hand up in front of your chest with the palm turned outward, the fingertips pointing to the left. Hold the left hand below the right in front of your stomach area, palm turned inward and fingertips pointing to the right. Now connect the thumbs and index fingers of both hands, creating the Wheel of Life. Hold for Three minutes and relax.

BREATH
LONG, DEEP AND SLOW THRU YOUR NOSE
MANTRA
OMM *(God in His Absolute State)*
AFFIRMATION
I AM BALANCED IN MY HEART, MIND AND BODY

Leopard Skin Jasper Sphere

Chapter Ten

Mudras & Crystals

ASTRAL PROTECTION SHIELD

Mudra for Astral Projection with Bridge & Barnacle Quartz

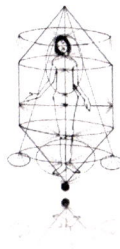

YOUR ASTRAL BODY IS YOUR DIVINE SHIELD

If you could easily see your fine energy body, you would most likely pay much greater attention to it. It would be quite startling to notice how negative thoughts create lingering dense clouds of blockages that bring your energy level down. On the other side of the spectrum, you would observe how love, happiness and positive thoughts magnify your energy field, make it glow and vibrate at its highest capacity. You would see the brilliant shine that spreads to those you love. You would be inspired by a beautiful and tangible shift every time you'd offer a helping hand or a kind word. It would be easy to understand and witness the immediate consequences of unhealthy behavior and consciously change your disposition. Many health challenges would be avoided, prevented and entirely eliminated. The beauty of compassion and love would outshine the tarnish of negativity. However, we live in a dimension that has certain limitations. Therefore the finer vibrations remain unseen by our human eyes. Nevertheless we remain very much affected by frequency shifts and changes. It is up to each one of us to make a conscious effort and sense beyond the invisible wall of limitations.

Your energy matrix is a complex subtle template that holds the vibrational imprint and information of your far away past, the present and all the possibilities for your future. You carry the gifts, desires as well as obstacles that will determine the path and success of your forthcoming life experiences.

Each one of us is forever connected to the magnificent and omni present Divine force. Our journeys onto the Earthly realm of human lifetimes are necessary and purposeful. Upon entering this world, our Soul memory is mostly unaccessible to us. This offers an opportunity for a clean and fresh start, while experiencing events with least resistance. With time, we may recall ancient far-away memories, but only to a certain extent. This "occasional glimpses" will help us remember, find and successfully pursue our purpose.

Your innermost desire is the greatest indicator of the mission and reason for your Earthly incarnation. Desires reveal your Soul's path as well as unresolved dynamics or relationships. Love never dies but propels you to return through ongoing future lifetimes. Strong emotions have powerful frequencies that permeate our entire being and drive our future actions, decisions and pursuits. The old longings and attachments are so persistent that they often bring us back into next incarnation in order to fulfill them. Following your desire will help you recognize and accomplish your mission. Your dreams are your navigation map to fulfilling your lifetime goals. If you ignore and deny your dreams and desires, they will not die, but simply retreat into a hiatus until you return in another life.

Understanding the importance and unavoidable power of your dreams is crucial. The final outcome of your quest is not as important as the actual opportunity to pursue your dreams. Often the path to fulfilling a dream reveals a true purpose that is much more impactful than the original goal itself. It is the journey that matters most, not the finish line.

Peach Selenite

If a person never has the opportunity to pursue a desire, they will always fell unfulfilled, subconsciously blaming others, situations or circumstances for their broken dreams. But if they allow themselves to give it a try, they may be perfectly content with the experience, and this may wholly suffice. Perhaps that is all they needed to experience and their desire is fulfilled. If someone dreams of fame and fortune, it will most likely result in their bittersweet realization that they chased after an illusion which will never bring them true happiness. Their desire may be fulfilled, but they will not experience the happiness they longed for. In time, they will realize the source of true happiness has nothing to do with seeking attention, adoration and validation from others.

Golden Healer Spirit Cactus

YOUR DREAMS AND DESIRES REVEAL YOUR LIFE MISSION. FOLLOW THEM.

We should all pursue our dreams. If it seems difficult or impossible, why not explore a simple version of your dream? You will soon know if this is truly something you want, or it is just an idea you are holding onto. The key to individual joy, contentment and happiness lies within your Soul. Accessing this information is the greatest gift one can receive. Fulfilling your desires will free you of Earthly chains. It will also propel you on your spiritual path of ascension.

No matter what your life's journey is, your belief system will pave the way. The core beliefs all lead to the ultimate ability of trust that you are guided, protected and loved by the Divine Power. This trust will offer comfort and inner peace as well as strength and confidence that your prayers for help will always be heard and you will never be deserted. One of our fundamental concerns is fear of abandonment in death. The unavoidable fact is that we all enter and depart this world seemingly alone. However, the realization and confidence that we are never truly alone, but always connected to the universal Divine power, can immediately diminish our fundamental fear and uplift us into a higher frequency. Faith that we are all interconnected, all part of One unifying force, such faith is an empowering key that will ultimately lead you to Self-actualization.

Your Astral Body is the connecting energy tier between the physical, mental, emotional subtle layers and the finer matrix templates of your being. Astral body is the last coating directly affected by the elements in your environment as well as people in it. In fact, there is much interaction on the Astral level with significant people in your life. This may remain entirely hidden from our Earthly eyes, but can definitely be sensed in a subtle way. Our Astral bodies communicate with each other on an entirely different level, as well as in our sleep. Your may experience dreams on the Astral level with your physical double - the Astral body.

YOUR ASTRAL BODY IS THE GATEWAY TO YOUR SPIRITUAL SELF. YOUR COMPLEX ENERGY FIELD HOLDS YOUR DETAILED AND MOST INTRICATE SOUL INFORMATION DATA.

When establishing your Energy protection shield for your Astral body, your trust in Divine is absolutely required. There should be no shadow of a doubt and no reluctant hesitation. However you relate to or visualize the Divine power is an entirely individual choice. Just know, your Spirit originates from an energy source that is unimaginably more infinite than your own. The love for you is boundless and you shall never be abandoned, no matter how dire the situation appears. Your home is in Eternity and your Soul is immortal. A conscious connection to the Higher Source is like having an open access to the command center that helps you navigate through unknown territories, foreign seas and dark skies.

YOU NEED EXPERT NAVIGATION, SUPREME GUIDANCE, AN UNEQUIVOCALLY RELIABLE ALLY AND OMNIPRESENT PROTECTOR ~ THE DIVINE FORCE. YOUR INDIVIDUAL ASTRAL SHIELD BELONGS TO THE INFINITE DIVINE SHIELD OF LIGHT.

Evoking and activating your Astral Shied requires a calm body, clear mind, open heart and the clarity of conscious intention. You also need mighty subtle energy power tools. Mudras and Crystals are your natural keys to grant you access to your Astral vessel.

To add more force to your Mudra and Crystal practice for Astral protection shield, add a powerful visualization component. Before you begin, get centered in your mind and with clear focus visualize a brilliant glowing Light that completely surrounds and permeates you. See it expand and vibrate with the power of love. Hold this image in your mind, unwavering and strong. With each inhalation, visualize your protective shield getting firmer and clearly outlined. When exhaling, release all negativity, doubt and fear. Inhale love and magnify the field, exhale all unneeded emotions. After the practice, stay in this visualized field and consciously close it off to any external elements.

Practice this visualization by calling upon this image every morning, before you leave your home, when you drive, or are in crowds surrounded by disruptive frequencies in your immediate setting. Train your mind to become fast and clear when you need immediate protection. Return to this image when you feel any doubts and remain strong, confident and crystal clear. Reinforce this shield before you go to sleep, so that your higher consciousness can facilitate and strengthen its effectiveness. Remember, the only person that can maintain your strong protective shield is YOU. However, your solid attunement with the Divine force will solidify and magnify your shield indefinitely. Mudras and Crystals will assist you to irrevocably seal the protective shield while maintaining its high frequency that is invulnerable and immune to disturbance.

With the Mudras presented in this chapter, the intention and focus is on establishing conscious connection with your Astral body and sealing a mighty energy shield with Divine love for your omnipresent protection.

Sunstone

Mudra for Divine Worship

Sit with a straight back and keep your shoulders down, nice and relaxed. Please a Crystal between the palms of your hands and join them together in front of your chest. If you are working with a Crystal wand, remember that whenever the Crystal is pointing away from you, the energy is directed outward. When Crystal is pointing toward you, the energy is directed inwards. Sit still and concentrate on your Third Eye for at least Three minutes.

BREATH
LONG, DEEP AND SLOW THRU YOUR NOSE
MANTRA
EK ONG KAR *(One Creator, God Is One)*
AFFIRMATION
I AM ONE WITH DIVINE FORCE, I AM PEACE

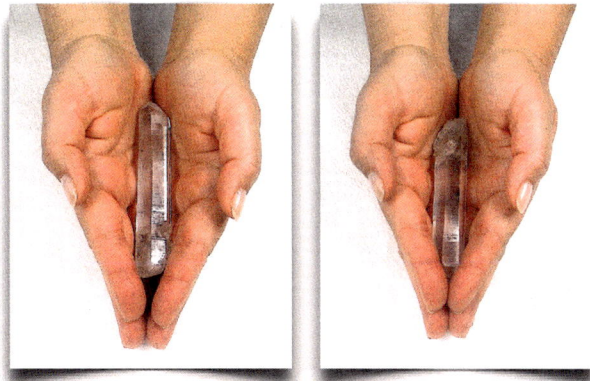

Mudra for Opening the Third Eye

Sit with a straight back and keep your shoulders down, nice and relaxed. Place a Crystal in your hands and hold it between the thumb and index fingers. Middle fingers are aligned with and touching the index fingers. The thumb tips, index and middle fingertips of both hands are touching. Extend the ring and little fingers and keep them apart. Lift your hands up and hold them in front of your Third Eye - Crown area. This Mudra is excellent for encoding and programming your Crystal. Hold for Three minutes and relax.

BREATH
Long, deep and slow thru your nose
MANTRA
OMM *(God in His Absolute State)*
AFFIRMATION
I OPEN MY SACRED WINDOW INTO INFINITY

MUDRA FOR FEELING YOUR ENERGY BODY

Sit with a straight back and keep your shoulders down, nice and relaxed. Select a medium size Crystal and place it in between your palms. Bring your hands in front of you, facing each other. The tips of the fingers are pointing away from you, all fingers are together. Keep a relaxed gaze on the area between your palms, without clearly focusing on the Crystal. An elongated Crystal is preferred, large enough to leave a small space between palms, so you can observe the subtle energy movement. Hold for Three minutes and relax.

BREATH
LONG, DEEP AND SLOW THRU YOUR NOSE
MANTRA
EK ONG KAR *(One Creator, God Is One)*
AFFIRMATION
I AM AN ENERGY FIELD OF LIGHT

MUDRA FOR ACTIVATING THE HEALING POWER IN YOUR HANDS

Sit with a straight back and keep your shoulders down, nice and relaxed. Take two small Crystals and hold them between your ring and thumb fingers - one in each hand. Lift the hands up to level of your head, palms facing forward. All other fingers are stretched out. Keep your elbows nice and high, away from your body. Hold for Three minutes and relax.

BREATH
LONG, DEEP AND SLOW THRU YOUR NOSE
MANTRA
SAT NAM *(Truth is God's name, One in Spirit))*
AFFIRMATION
I ACTIVATE THE HEALING FORCE IN MY HANDS

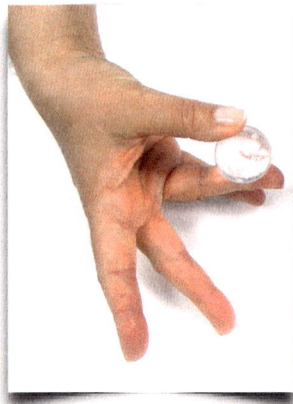

Mudra for Powerful insight

    Sit with a straight back and keep your shoulders down, nice and relaxed. Place a Crystal in the palm of your left hand, and make a gentle fist. Bend your elbows and raise your hands to the level of the navel. Hold your left hand up, palm turned up towards the sky and place it into the palm of your right hand. Concentrate on your Third Eye, breathe, and hold for Three minutes.

BREATH
LONG, DEEP AND SLOW THRU YOUR NOSE

MANTRA
SAT NAM *(Truth is God's name, One in Spirit))*

AFFIRMATION
I CALL UPON MY INSIGHT AND DISCERNMENT

Mudra for Heightened Awareness

Sit with a straight back and keep your shoulders down, nice and relaxed. Place a Crystal between your palms and lift your hands above your head. Palms are pressed together, elbows to the side. Inhale, stretch your elbows and raise your hands as if someone is pulling them up. Then exhale, bend your elbows and lower your hands to a position of a few inches above your head, palms always pressed together. Repeat for Three minutes.

BREATH
INHALE SLOWLY WHEN LIFTING HANDS, EXHALE WHEN LOWERING HANDS
MANTRA
SAT NAM *(Truth Is God's Name, One in Spirit)*
AFFIRMATION
I RAISE MY AWARENESS, I REACH FOR THE LIGHT

Mudra for Higher Consciousness

Sit with a straight back, shoulders down, nice and relaxed. Place a Crystal between the palms of your hands. Lift your hands to the solar plexus level, keep your palms together, fingers pointing away from you. Tuck your thumbs under so that their tips rest on the fleshy mounds below your little fingers. The Crystal sits in the small space in your palms. Your hands are touching firmly, your elbows are to the side. Practice for Three minutes.

BREATH
Long, deep and slow thru your nose

MANTRA
OMM *(God in His Absolute State)*

AFFIRMATION
I HAVE ACCESS TO MY HIGHER KNOWLEDGE

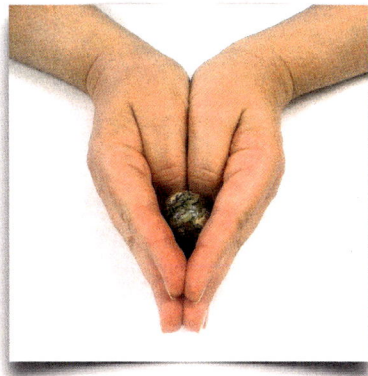

MUDRA FOR CREATIVITY

Sit with a straight back, shoulders down, nice and relaxed. Place one or a few small Crystals into the center of each palm. Connect the thumbs and index fingertips, keeping the rest of the fingers straight and together. Bend your elbows and lift your hands to your sides with palms facing up at a sixty-degree angle to your body. The Crystals are sitting in your palms. Concentrate on your Third Eye center and meditate for at least Three minutes.

BREATH
SHORT, FAST BREATH OR FIRE FROM THE NAVEL
MANTRA
GA DA *(God) variation elbows in or out 60 degree*
AFFIRMATION
I AM CREATIVELY INSPIRED, INVENTIVE AND ORIGINAL

MUDRA FOR INVISIBILITY

Sit with a straight back and keep your shoulders down, nice and relaxed. Place a Crystal in your right hand and hold it in a gentle fist. Lift up the hand so your palm is facing toward you. Now hold the left hand above your right fist, palm facing down, all fingers straight and together. The hands are not touching. If you are using a Crystal wand, point the tip towards the ground. Practice for Three minutes.

BREATH
LONG, DEEP AND SLOW THRU YOUR NOSE
MANTRA
OMM *(God in His Absolute State)*
AFFIRMATION
I AM SUBTLY IMPERCEPTIBLE AND PROTECTED

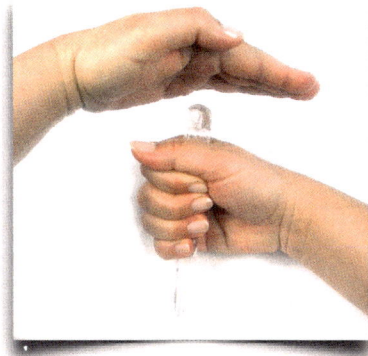

MUDRA FOR EVOKING A SACRED SCENT OF PERFUME

Sit with a straight back, shoulders down, nice and relaxed. Place a Crystal in your left hand and hold it in a gentle fist. Lift the left hand and hold it in front of your chest, palm turned towards you. Lift your right hand, palm open and facing the knuckles of your left hand. With the flat lower part of your fingers of the left hand, press your fist against the palm of your right hand. Apply gentle pressure and hold. When practicing this Mudra in high state of meditation, you will sense a sacred scent. Practice for Three minutes.

BREATH
LONG, DEEP AND SLOW THRU YOUR NOSE
MANTRA
OMM *(God in His Absolute State)*
AFFIRMATION
MY EXTRA SENSORY PERCEPTION IS ABUNDANT

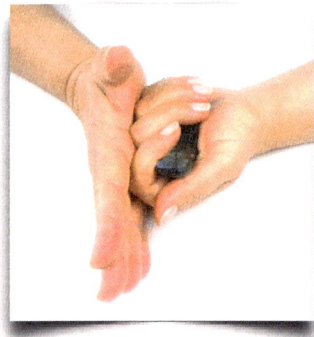

Mudra for Expanding Perspective

Sit with a straight back and keep your shoulders down, nice and relaxed. Place a Crystal in your right hand. Lift both hands up and hold them under your chin, without actually touching your chin. The right hand is on top of the left hand, both facing the ground. The Crystal is resting in space under the right palm on top of the left hand. Elbows are held lightly to the side. Practice for Three minutes.

BREATH
LONG, DEEP AND SLOW THRU YOUR NOSE
MANTRA
SAT NAM *(Truth Is God's Name, One in Spirit)*
AFFIRMATION
I EXPAND AND BROADEN MY PERSPECTIVE

MUDRA FOR CALLING THE GODS OF THE EARTH

Sit with a straight back, shoulders down, nice and relaxed. Place a Crystal in the palm of your left hand, keep the palm open and facing up, towards the sky. Bend your elbows and position your left hand at your solar plexus level. Keep the fingers together. Place a Crystal wand into your right hand, bring it level with your left, palm facing your body, and point the right index finger and Crystal wand down towards the Earth. Practice for Three minutes.

BREATH
LONG, DEEP AND SLOW THRU YOUR NOSE
MANTRA
OMM *(God in His Absolute State)*
AFFIRMATION
I CALL ON THE GODS OF THE EARTH FOR PROTECTION

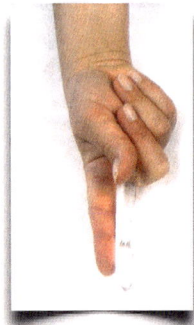

Mudra for Evoking Your Intuitive Voice

Sit with a straight back and keep your shoulders down, nice and relaxed. Place a Crystal in the palms of your hands and intertwine your fingers leaving the index fingers straight and pressed against each other at full length. Bend your elbows and lift your hands up, hold them at the level of your throat with outstretched index fingers in front of, but not touching your lips. Index fingers point up towards the sky, thumbs are crossed. Practice for Three minutes.

BREATH
LONG, DEEP AND SLOW THRU YOUR NOSE

MANTRA
OMM *(God in His Absolute State)*

AFFIRMATION
I CALL ON MY INTUITION

MUDRA FOR RECEIVING UNIVERSE'S LAW

Sit with a straight back and keep your shoulders down, nice and relaxed. Place a Crystal into the palm of your left hand. Lift your left hand to your solar plexus area, palm facing up, toward the sky. Lift the right hand to heart level, palm facing down, right above the left hand. Leave enough space between the palms for a small ball. Elbows are to the side. All fingers on both hands are together and stretched, hands are lightly cupped. Hold the Mudra and concentrate on the energy between your palms. Practice for Three minutes.

BREATH
LONG, DEEP AND SLOW THRU YOUR NOSE
MANTRA
OMM *(God in His Absolute State)*
AFFIRMATION
I RESPECT AND RECEIVE THE LAWS OF THE UNIVERSE

MUDRA FOR EVOKING THE POWER OF JUPITER

Sit with a straight back and keep your shoulders down, nice and relaxed. Place a Crystal into the palm of your right hand and hold it in a gentle fist, leaving index - Jupiter finger out and straight, pointing up to the sky. If you are using a Crystal wand, make sure the tip is pointing upwards. Bend the left arm and place the right elbow into the cupped left hand. With the upper part of the right arm, begin making counter-clockwise circles, two revolutions per inhale and two revolutions per exhale. Feel the vortex of energy as you spin your right upper arm. You are evoking the qualities of Jupiter which are good fortune, abundance, prosperity, expansion and healing. Practice for Three minutes and relax.

BREATH
LONG, DEEP AND SLOW THRU YOUR NOSE
MANTRA
SAT NAM *(Truth Is God's Name, One in Spirit)*
AFFIRMATION
I CALL UPON JUPITER FOR GIFTS OF GOOD FORTUNE

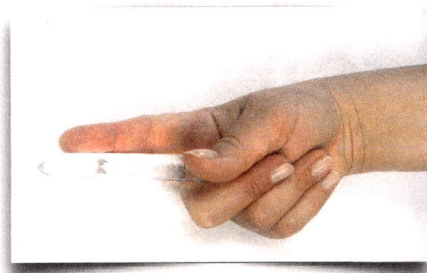

MUDRA FOR CLARITY OF DECISION

Sit with a straight back, your shoulders down, nice and relaxed. Place a smaller Crystal in each hand and gently fold your thumbs over them to keep them in place. The rest of your fingers are straight and together. Lift your hands up to the sides of your head while directing the palms towards your upper face and forehead. You are not touching your face, but holding an energy shield, helping you remove distractions and gain clarity. This Mudra is different from *Mudra for Looking into the Future*. Here palms are turned towards your upper face and forehead. Practice for Three minutes and relax.

BREATH
LONG, DEEP AND SLOW THRU YOUR NOSE
MANTRA
SAT NAM *(Truth Is God's Name, One in Spirit)*
AFFIRMATION
I AM CLEAR, DIRECT AND ACCURATE IN MY DECISIONS

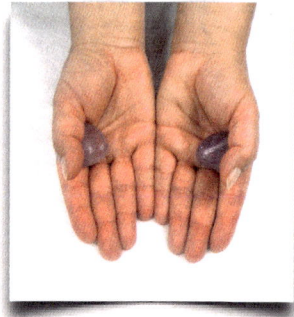

Mudra for Closing~off Your Aura

    Sit with a straight back and keep your shoulders down, nice and relaxed. Place a medium size Crystal in your hands. Bend your middle, ring and small fingers. Both index and thumb fingertips are connected. The Crystals is resting on thumbs, in the space between the bent thumbs and middle finger knuckles of both hands. Lift your hands up to the level of your throat so that the Crystal is facing you. Hold for Three minutes and relax.

BREATH
LONG, DEEP AND SLOW THRU YOUR NOSE
MANTRA
OMM *(God in His Absolute State)*
AFFIRMATION
I CLOSE OFF MY AURA
MY INVISIBLE ENERGY SHIELD IS INDESTRUCTIBLE

Mudra for Awakening your Divine potential

Sit with a straight back and keep your shoulders down, nice and relaxed. Place a Crystal in each hand, wrap your fingers around each one of them and leave your outstretched thumbs outside of the fist. Bend your elbows, lift up your arms in front of your chest and press your forearms together all the way from your elbows to your wrists. The knuckles of both hands are touching, thumbs are pointing up towards the sky. When using Crystal wands, point their tips upwards. Hold for Three minutes and relax.

BREATH
LONG, DEEP AND SLOW THRU YOUR NOSE
MANTRA
OMM *(God in His Absolute State)*
AFFIRMATION
I AWAKEN MY OPTIMAL DIVINE POTENTIAL

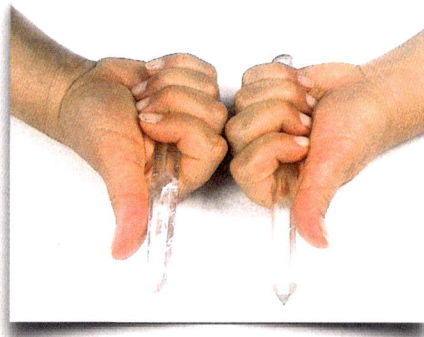

MUDRA FOR MAGNIFYING PERCEPTION

    Sit with a straight back, shoulders down, nice and relaxed. Place a smaller size Crystal in each hand, wrap your middle, ring, and little fingers around them into a gentle fists. Stretch the index and thumb fingers of both hands and connect the thumb and index fingertips. Bend your elbows and lift your hands up to the level of your face, and direct the gaze of your right eye through the opening in your hands. This Mudra is different from *Mudra for Closing-off Your Aura*. Here, hands are at face level, eyes are open. Hold for Three minutes and relax.

BREATH
LONG, DEEP AND SLOW THRU YOUR NOSE
MANTRA
OMM *(God in His Absolute State)*
AFFIRMATION
MY PERCEPTION IS EXPANDING AND INCREASING

Mudra Set for Crossing all Adversities

This Mudra Set will activate and empower your self-sustaining power from within. During the practice the rhythm and flow of energy polarity is balanced, and your ability to overcome all obstacles and adversities is magnified in a most auspicious way.

Sit with a straight back and keep your shoulders down, nice and relaxed. Place a medium size Crystal into the center of your palms. Lift your hands up to the level of your upper chest and join the hands at the wrists. Your thumbs are aligned side by side, stretched and pointing towards you. Your small fingers are stretched, fingertips touching and pointing away from you. All other fingers are stretched and not touching. The hands form a shape of a Lotus flower blossom opening and closing.

This Mudra is practiced with a mantra.
Practice as follows:
Chant the mantra **SA** audibly while the thumbs and little finger tips touch.
Chant the mantra **TA** audibly and join the ring fingertips.
Chant the mantra **NA** audibly and join the middle fingertips.
Chant the mantra **MA** audibly and join the index fingertips.

Now open your hands to original position and repeat the entire sequence in a WHISPER.
Lastly, practice the entire sequence in SILENCE.
Now practice the entire sequence and return to a WHISPER.
Finally repeat the entire sequence again AUDIBLY.
Practice for **Eleven minutes**.

BREATH
LONG, DEEP AND SLOW THRU YOUR NOSE

MANTRA
SA TA NA MA
(Infinity Life, Death, Rebirth)

SA
CONNECTING LITTLE
FINGERTIPS AND THUMB TIPS

TA
CONNECTING RING FINGER TIPS

NA
CONNECTING MIDDLE FINGERTIPS

MA
CONNECTING INDEX FINGERTIPS

Smokey Citrine Quartz Polished Point

ABOUT THE AUTHOR

SABRINA MESKO Ph.D.H. is a recognized Mudra authority and International and Los Angeles Times bestselling author of the timeless classic *Healing Mudras - Yoga for your Hands* translated into fourteen languages. She authored over twenty books on Mudras, Mudra Therapy, Mudras and Astrology, and meditation techniques.

Sabrina was born in Europe where she became a classical ballerina at an early age. In her teens she moved to New York and became a principal Broadway dancer and singer who turned to yoga to heal a back injury. Eastern-trained but Western-based, she completed a several-year intensive study of teachings with world renowned Masters, one of whom entrusted her with bringing the sacred Mudra techniques to the West. She is a Yoga College of India certified Yoga Therapist.

Sabrina holds a Bachelors Degree in Sensory Approaches to Healing, a Masters in Holistic Science, and a Doctorate in Ancient and Modern Approaches to Healing from the American Institute of Holistic Theology. She is board certified from the American Alternative medical Association and American Holistic Health Association.

She has been featured in media outlets such as The Los Angeles Times, CNBC News, Cosmopolitan, the cover of London Times Lifestyle, The Discovery Channel documentary on Hands, W magazine, First for Women, Health, Web- MD, Daily News, Focus, Yoga Journal, Australian Women's weekly, Blend, Daily Breeze, New Age, the Roseanne Show and various international live television programs. Her articles have been published in world-wide publications. She hosted her own weekly TV show educating about health, well-being and complementary medicine. She is an executive member of the World Yoga Council and has led numerous international Yoga Therapy educational programs. She directed and produced her interactive double DVD titled *Chakra Mudras* - a Visionary awards finalist. Sabrina also created award winning international Spa and Wellness Centers and is a motivational keynote conference speaker addressing large audiences all over the world. Sabrina recently launched Arnica Press, a boutique Book Publishing House. Her mission is to discover, mentor, nurture and publish unique authors with a meaningful message, that may otherwise not have an opportunity to be heard.

She is the founder of MUDRA MASTERY ™ the world's only online Mudra Teacher and Mudra Therapy Education, Certification, and Mentorship program, with her certified graduates and therapists spreading these ancient teachings in over 26 countries around the world.

WWW.SABRINAMESKO.COM

Vivianite Blade resting on a Golden Healer Quartz Barnacle

Made in the USA
Monee, IL
24 October 2022